The Influence Workout

PEARSON

At Pearson, we believe in learning – all kinds of learning for all kinds of people. Whether it's at home, in the classroom or in the workplace, learning is the key to improving our life chances.

That's why we're working with leading authors to bring you the latest thinking and best practices, so you can get better at the things that are important to you. You can learn on the page or on the move, and with content that's always crafted to help you understand quickly and apply what you've learned.

If you want to upgrade your personal skills or accelerate your career, become a more effective leader or more powerful communicator, discover new opportunities or simply find more inspiration, we can help you make progress in your work and life.

Pearson is the world's leading learning company. Our portfolio includes the Financial Times and our education business, Pearson International.

Every day our work helps learning flourish, and wherever learning flourishes, so do people.

To learn more, please visit us at **www.pearson.com/uk**

The Influence Workout

The 10 tried-and-tested steps that will build your influencing power

David Windle and Guy Michaels

PEARSON

Harlow, England • London • New York • Boston • San Francisco • Toronto • Sydney
Auckland • Singapore • Hong Kong • Tokyo • Seoul • Taipei • New Delhi
Cape Town • São Paulo • Mexico City • Madrid • Amsterdam • Munich • Paris • Milan

Pearson Education Limited
Edinburgh Gate
Harlow CM20 2JE
United Kingdom
Tel: +44 (0)1279 623623
Web: www.pearson.com/uk

First published 2015 (print and electronic)

© Pearson Education Limited 2015 (print and electronic)

The rights of David Windle and Guy Michaels to be identified as authors of this work has been asserted by them in accordance with the Copyright, Designs and Patents Act 1988.

Pearson Education is not responsible for the content of third-party internet sites.

ISBN: 978-1-292-01713-6 (print)
    978-1-292-01715-0 (PDF)
    978-1-292-01716-7 (ePub)
    978-1-292-01714-3 (eText)

British Library Cataloguing-in-Publication Data
A catalogue record for the print edition is available from the British Library

Library of Congress Cataloging-in-Publication Data
Windle, David.
  The influence workout / David Windle and Guy Michaels.
    pages cm
  ISBN 978-1-292-01713-6 (print) — ISBN 978-1-292-01715-0 (PDF) -- ISBN 978-1-292-01716-7 (ePub) — ISBN 978-1-292-01714-3 (eText)
  1. Influence (Psychology) 2. Persuasion (Psychology) I. Michaels, Guy. II. Title.
  BF774.W56 2015
  358.4'092—dc23
                                                                    2015005339

10 9 8 7 6 5 4 3 2 1
19 18 17 16 15

Print edition typeset in 10/13 Scene Std by 71
Print edition printed and bound in Great Britain by Henry Ling Ltd, at the Dorset Press, Dorchester, Dorset

NOTE THAT ANY PAGE CROSS REFERENCES REFER TO THE PRINT EDITION

Contents

Examine the key relationships you have at work and home and understand what gives you influence in them. Place those key stakeholders on the 'engagement scale.' Recognise the wider-reaching ripples of influence that you have, and the limits of your influence.

Learn to use your body to convey the influence and impact you wish to have. Understand how we 'give ourselves away' and undermine our influence by having weak non-verbal habits. Learn to use your body to give you greater confidence and command.

What makes a voice effective? Learn the skills of the greatest speakers to ensure that your voice carries the right impact and makes the best connection with your

Contents

Putting it into action (the mentor toolkit)   161

How to work with a manager or colleague to put your new skills
into action

Self-assessment questionnaire   169

What have you learnt?
What can you put into practice today?
How will you do it?

Index   172

About the authors

David Windle and **Guy Michaels** formed Opposite Leg Training in 2006. Since then they have presented at conferences and designed training programmes for a wide range of clients from global organisations to the freshest of start-ups. They regularly provide one-to-one coaching for senior executives, helping them boost their impact and presence.

Their communication and presentation skills training are never a lecture; they are always playful and interactive, leaving trainees buzzing and motivated to try out their new skills.

Find out more about them and their work at:
www.oppositeleg.co.uk

Acknowledgements

We would like to thank the following people for their support and contributions throughout the writing of *The Influence Workout*:

Dr. Peter Windle

Hayley Eaton

Emma Smith

Basil Eaton

Pamela Thompson

Christine Windle

Gus Tompkins

Trisha Beausaert

Stamos Fafalios

Richard Halsall

Vicky Annand

Louis Barbe

Andrew Plender

Fiona Dawe

Ana Canabarro

Annabelle Roberts

Ian Finch

Joanna Holmes

Finally, to our editor at Pearson, Eloise Cook: thank you for guiding us through the publishing world.

Publisher's acknowledgements

Pearson would like to thank the following for their help in developing *The Influence Workout*:

Richard Barnard

Bob Bates

Shohil Bhudia

Mike Brent

Jacq Burns

Karen Campbell-White

Lucy Carter

Sian Choudhury

Kosta Christofi

Guy Clapperton

Daniel Clayden

Mike Clayton

Darren Clegg

Brigitte Cobb

Cyrus Cooper

Toril Cooper

David Cox

Ian Coyne

John Dembitz

Alex Dennis

Fiona Dent

Gersy Ejimofo

Fadi El-Sayed

Mark Fearnley

Donna Goddard

Euan Grant

Adam Gray

Sharon Grove

Edouard Gruwez

Rebecca Harvey

Ian Hazon

Michael Heppell

Malcolm Hornby

Bruce Hoverd

Mechthild Huelsmann

Pat Hutchinson

James Innes

Karl James

Amy Joyner

John Kelly

Leif Kendall

Madeleine Kershaw

Harry Key

Annie Lionnet

Chris Locke

Jonquil Lowe

Publisher's acknowledgements

Steven Mackenzie
Bernard Marr
Kelly Miller
Lisa Mintzberg
Erica Minuzzo
Nathalie Morris
Jenny Nabben
Zo Neufville
Richard Norris
Fergus O'Connell
Paul Pietersma
Emma-Sue Prince
John Purkiss
Steven Reynolds
Marc Rhodes
Chris Robson
Ray Rowlings
Gregory Savi

Caroline Scherrer
Julie Starr
Robbie Steinhouse
Georgie Stone
Shchenkova Svetlana
Shirley Taylor
Elizabeth Thomas
Jordan Thomas
Heather Townsend
Ken Trim
Sarah Turpie
Amanda Vickers
Antonio Weiss
Anthea Willey
John Williams
Jurgen Wolff
Caspian Woods

Text credits

We are grateful to the following for permission to reproduce copyright material:

Dictionary extracts on page xv are reproduced from Cambridge Dictionaries Online (dictionary.cambridge.org/) © Cambridge University Press

In some instances we have been unable to trace the owners of copyright material, and we would appreciate any information that would enable us to do so.

Picture credits

The publisher also would like to thank the following for their kind permission to reproduce their photographs:

(Key: b-bottom; c-centre; l-left; r-right; t-top)

Page xiv: Bridgeman Art Library Ltd: The North Wind and the Sun, illustration from 'Aesop's Fables', published by Heinemann, 1912 (colour litho), Rackham, Arthur (1867-1939) / Private Collection.

Page 7: David Windle and Guy Michaels; 11: Shutterstock.com: michaeljung (l, c, r); 12: Alamy Images: Pictorial Press Ltd; 14: Alamy Images: Masa Ushioda; 17: Rex Features: Eddie Mulholland; 39: Shutterstock.com: Garsya; 48: Getty Images: Photo by CBS; 55: Royston Robertson: www.roystoncartoons.com; 62: TopFoto: John Topham; 63: Rex Features: Nils Jorgensen; 66: Alamy Images: Pictorial Press Ltd; 71: Shutterstock.com: Jeanne Provost; 86: David Windle and Guy Michaels; 89: Alamy Images: Only Horses Tbk; 97: Getty Images: Oli Scarff; 99: Alamy Images: Uppercut Images; 106: Rex Features: Canadian Press; 109: Shutterstock. com: FotomanufakturZ; 118: Alamy Images: Nurlan Kalchinov; 119: David Windle and Guy Michaels.

All other images © Pearson Education

Every effort has been made to trace the copyright holders and we apologise in advance for any unintentional omissions. We would be pleased to insert the appropriate acknowledgement in any subsequent edition of this publication.

The Wind and the Sun

THE NORTH WIND AND THE SUN

The Wind and the Sun were disputing which was the stronger. Suddenly they saw a traveller coming down the road, and the Sun said: 'I see a way to decide our dispute. Whichever of us can cause that traveller to take off his cloak shall be regarded as the stronger. You begin.' So the Sun retired behind a cloud, and the Wind began to blow as hard as it could upon the traveller. But the harder he blew the more closely did the traveller wrap his cloak round him, until at last the Wind had to give up in despair. Then the Sun came out and shone in all his glory upon the traveller, who soon found it too hot to walk with his cloak on.

Introduction

What is influence?

Influence (*noun*) the power to have an effect on people or things.[1]

Influence (*verb*) to affect or change how someone or something develops, behaves or thinks.[2]

What could be simpler? Go on, get out there and use your power of influence to change the way someone behaves. What are you waiting for?

But it's not that easy, is it? (No it isn't . . . and anyone who pretends otherwise is just trying to influence the way you think about them.)

Luckily, this book provides the concepts and skills needed to set you in the right direction and help you harness your power of influence.

The good thing about having a verb version of 'influence' to play with is that anyone can learn to do a verb, even if it takes a while.

In short, it is what we *do* that makes us influential and *leads* us to have the power to affect people.

This book focusses on the things you need to think about and, crucially, *do* to be influential.

[1]Cambridge Dictionaries Online (http://dictionary.cambridge.org/dictionary/business-english/influence_2)

[2]Cambridge Dictionaries Online (http://dictionary.cambridge.org/dictionary/british/influence)

Remember these skills are *soft skills*; a soft skill can sometimes be as simple as a new angle of approach, a change of focus or a broader awareness.

None of the ideas in this book is a fixed technique to be applied without thought and reflection. Every influencing situation is different and no single formula will solve them all.

Our aim is to set you up with a broad range of concepts and tools to ensure that you are as flexible and adept an influencer as possible.

Why do you want it?

Maybe you don't want to be influential, you're just happy with a low profile. Not everyone wants to be president. Maybe you want it so much you're kept awake at night by fevered dreams of world domination?

Or maybe, like most of us, you're somewhere in between.

The thing is, in the world of work, you can't really avoid having an influence, whether you like it or not. We all influence each other on a daily basis, from our first interactions at the coffee counter, to senior meetings in the boardroom. Your behaviour defines the impact you have on yourself and your stakeholders.

And everyone is a stakeholder. Every single person you interact with both influences you and is influenced by you to some degree, no matter how small.

Given that, it's definitely a good idea to employ some good influencing habits and ensure you are making the right impression.

The key principles

Our three key principles for being influential:

1. prepare yourself;
2. maintain relationships;
3. communicate clearly.

The good thing about neat principles like this is that they serve as a simple reminder of the things you need to do to keep your levels of influence on an upward path. So remember them. Right now.

The danger with neat principles like this is that things are never as simple as a principle suggests, so don't be fooled into thinking you don't need to work hard to make them happen.

Principle 1: Prepare yourself

You can only be purposefully influential if you have prepared the ground. And the ground is you and your inner world: what you stand for, what your aim is and why it matters. Your inner world defines what you communicate and the messages you give. It is essential to sort this out.

Principle 2: Maintain relationships

Without relationships, you have no influence. Your relationships are the channels through which you are able to affect people. It's a two-way street, and the nature of these relationships defines the nature of the influence you have. Of course, most of our lives are an interconnecting web of different relationships that function in different ways. In short, no one set of influencing rules works: you need to be flexible.

Principle 3: Communicate clearly

Once you've worked out what you're all about, and examined the relationships you need to nurture, the next step is to make sure that what you say and do gives out the right signal.

If your signal is muddled, your influence is weak.

How this book works

This book gives you the *soft skills* and ideas you need to put these three guiding principles into practice.

The first 10 steps set you up with the skills you need to be an expert influencer, ensuring you have the techniques and awareness needed to wield your influence with panache and dexterity.

But it's not all theory!

Inside each of the first 10 steps there are exercises and skills tests to try out, guaranteeing that you embed the learning in your brain and body. Influencing is a practical skill and needs to be learnt through *doing*; you can't just read a book about it!

Once you've read the first 10 steps, the remaining two parts of the book reveal how to apply these skills in real-life situations, giving you expert tips on how to maximise your influence when it really matters.

You can read this book from cover to cover or dip in and out as you please.

It's the complete influencing toolkit.

You'll notice three icons highlighting either an **Activity**, what we regard as a **Key idea**, or additional **Media** content. The icons we will use are:

Activity   **Key idea**   **Media**

Self-assessment questionnaire

Do this questionnaire before you begin the book and training programme to gain a quick overview of your current influencing skills and your confidence using them.

Score yourself 1–10 for each of these questions: 10 indicates a high level of confidence and skill and 1 a low level:

1. How influential do you feel at work?

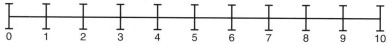

2. How influential do you feel at home?

3. How well do you understand your universe of influence/ network of relationships?

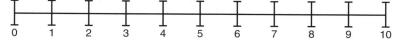

4. How comfortable are you using non-verbal communication?

5. How confident are you in the sound of your voice?

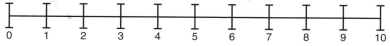

6. **How comfortable are you when presenting to an audience?**

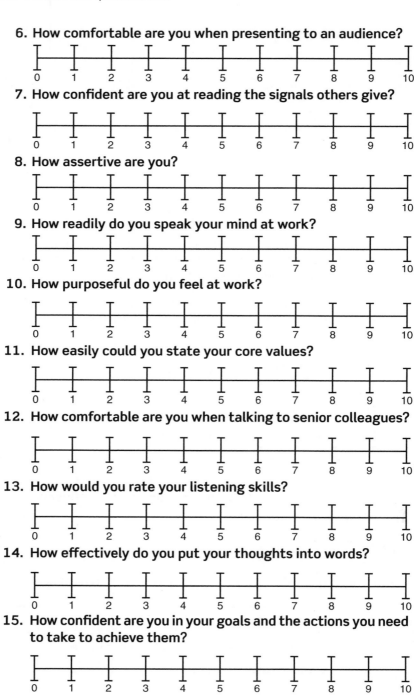

```
0   1   2   3   4   5   6   7   8   9   10
```

7. **How confident are you at reading the signals others give?**

```
0   1   2   3   4   5   6   7   8   9   10
```

8. **How assertive are you?**

```
0   1   2   3   4   5   6   7   8   9   10
```

9. **How readily do you speak your mind at work?**

```
0   1   2   3   4   5   6   7   8   9   10
```

10. **How purposeful do you feel at work?**

```
0   1   2   3   4   5   6   7   8   9   10
```

11. **How easily could you state your core values?**

```
0   1   2   3   4   5   6   7   8   9   10
```

12. **How comfortable are you when talking to senior colleagues?**

```
0   1   2   3   4   5   6   7   8   9   10
```

13. **How would you rate your listening skills?**

```
0   1   2   3   4   5   6   7   8   9   10
```

14. **How effectively do you put your thoughts into words?**

```
0   1   2   3   4   5   6   7   8   9   10
```

15. **How confident are you in your goals and the actions you need to take to achieve them?**

```
0   1   2   3   4   5   6   7   8   9   10
```

Once you have read the book, completed all the exercises more than once and spent some time working on the techniques with a training partner/mentor, then do the questionnaire again and notice in which areas you have developed significantly and which still require attention.

 Watch an animation to learn more about the three principles for successful influence:

www.thebusinessgym.net

Part 1

10 steps to greater influence

Step 1

Relationships – understand your sphere of influence

After reading this step you will be able to:

- Identify your sphere of influence
- Recognise the importance of relationships for influence
- Identify the relationships where your influence could be greater
- Improve your power of influence through relationships.

Simply put, a relationship is the way in which two people connect. And, it is the *way* in which you are connected to any other person that shapes the influence you have upon them and they have upon you.

You only have to think back to your time at school and bring to mind the teachers who had the greatest impact upon you, to realise that it was the nature of their relationships with you that gave them their powers of influence.

There are probably also a host of teachers you can barely recall, precisely because they had no particular relationship with you.

These relationships can be defined in many different ways and, therefore, carry influence in many different ways. Mr Smith may have had influence because he was empathetic and interested in what motivated you to learn; whereas Ms Jones may have influenced you by setting high academic expectations and providing the in-depth subject knowledge you needed to scrape that top grade at A-level.

 Each relationship has its own shape, and carries influence in its own way.

This all sounds rather obvious, doesn't it? Which is why it is so easy to take your relationships for granted.

The first step to greater influence is to audit your relationships. Here's how.

How to do it

Do a relationship audit

A relationship audit is a big picture snapshot of your universe of influence, which enables you to quickly map out your key stakeholders. Once you've drawn your map you'll easily be able to spot both the relationships in need of nurture and those which may be suffering undue strain.

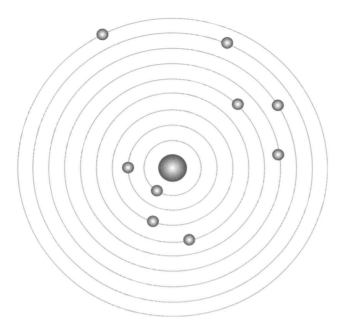

You are the centre of your unique universe, and you are surrounded by other celestial bodies (planets, stars, black holes – stakeholders of all kinds!). Some of these celestial bodies are well within your orbit; others barely feel the pull of your fading gravity across the great chasm of space.

Some of the bodies in your universe may exert huge gravitational force upon you while you have little influence over them and vice versa.

The key is that the influence always works on a two-way basis; everything in your universe has some kind of relationship to you.

Luckily this universe doesn't obey the normal laws of physics as, once you've drawn your map, you can then begin the process of increasing your gravitational effect on even the most distant star.

Let's get to work.

Draw your universe of influence

Grab an A4 piece of paper.

Draw this on it:

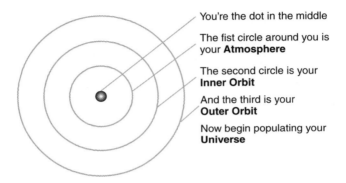

You're the dot in the middle

The fist circle around you is your **Atmosphere**

The second circle is your **Inner Orbit**

And the third is your **Outer Orbit**

Now begin populating your **Universe**

Universe of influence

1. Name all the people who exist in your immediate atmosphere – those who are profoundly affected by your gravity. These people may be from your personal and your work lives.

2. Move to circle 2 and identify all those people who fall within your orbit, with whom you interact on a regular basis, and with whom you have some interdependency. Again, they can be from any area of your life.

3. In circle 3, identify those people, or organisations, who do not greatly feel your gravity. They may or may not exert a heavy pull upon you in return.

4. Now draw a line connecting each person on your map to you. On one side of the line score the strength of your gravitational pull on that person out of 10. On the other side, give a score out of 10 for the strength of their effect upon you. It's a good idea to use different-coloured pens for this!

5. After this, scan the relationships on your map and notice where there is greatest disparity between the ratings. This will indicate where you need to focus your attention.

Draw your universe of influence right now with the help of a video:

www.thebusinessgym.net

The areas of greatest imbalance are weak points in your universe of influence. If you wield a huge influence over a stakeholder, yet they feel powerless, this isn't sustainable; equally, if someone wields great influence over you, yet you have no say, you'll soon become disengaged.

Take a piggyback ride!

Another useful tactic at this stage is to make further connections between your stakeholders, spotting opportunities to take a piggyback ride. If Stakeholder A exerts a strong influence over more distant Stakeholder B, by developing your alliance with Stakeholder A, you will gradually be able to draw Stakeholder B deeper into your orbit.

This map gives you a big-picture overview of your universe of influence, enabling you to think strategically long term.

Universe zoom

Case study

A major UK charity asked us to analyse some communication difficulties occurring in its marketing team. It didn't take long to realise that there were huge imbalances in the relationships present within the team, and most of these imbalances stemmed from the differing personalities of two bosses.

Boss 1, Darren, managed one set of donor accounts and boss 2, Rob, managed another, and the rest of the marketing team were responsible for meeting both Darren and Rob's needs. The trouble was, Darren's needs were always met on time and with great diligence, whereas Rob's requests were left unattended until the last minute and only then answered with a side serving of disgruntlement.

The reason was simple: the quality of the relationships the respective bosses had with their immediate stakeholders.

Rob chose to sit at a desk at the opposite end of the office from his colleagues. He rarely communicated with them in person, other than when he summoned them to his desk demanding a progress check. All the staff mentioned the dread they felt whenever they took the slow walk to Rob's desk. His emails were abrupt, his presence at meetings severe and he never offered any encouragement. In short, the defining features of his relationships were fear and distrust.

Darren, on the other hand, chose to sit at a desk in the midst of the team, separated only by a partition, over which his head would regularly pop to chivvy his colleagues along. Darren showed interest in and curiosity about the lives of his staff outside of work, he joined in the office banter and sometimes even made the coffee! However, he also managed to command a healthy level of respect; no one was left in any doubt if a piece of work was not up to scratch. Needless to say, Darren's colleagues were keen to support him to the best of their abilities.

This extreme, yet simple, example demonstrates how important the nature of your relationships is in determining the nature of your influence, and highlights why it is always essential to reflect upon how you manage your most important relationships.

 **Exercise**

Once you have completed your universe of influence map, select three stakeholders with whom you have noticed that there is an imbalance in the power of influence ratings between you and them.

It may be useful to take a stakeholder from each circle of your map, as they can present quite different challenges. For example, a close colleague over whom you have little influence needs to be approached in a very different way from an external service provider.

Then, for each of your three selected stakeholders, consider the main barriers that hamper your influence with them and decide on three practical steps that you can take over the next weeks to begin enhancing your influence.

It may be as simple as going via the stakeholder's desk in the morning, or inviting them to an event. Or it could be more strategic: begin reading up about their area of knowledge and participating in the forums and discussion groups they appear in; or connect on social media.

The key is to take small, but practical, steps forward.

Call to action

- Can you identify your key stakeholders?
- Can you place them on your universe of influence map?
- Have you identified the relationships that experience the greatest levels of imbalance between your level of influence and the stakeholders?
- Have you considered how you can begin to tackle these imbalances?
- Have you spotted any opportunities to piggyback?

Step 2

The body of influence – non-verbal impact

After reading this step you will be able to:

- Let your body and breathing support your communication
- Interpret and use the non-verbal cues worth worrying about
- Focus on the space between people
- Allow your body to lead your brain.

If you stacked one copy of every book on body language published in the past decade on top of another, your stack would be taller than the Empire State Building. Probably.

Suffice it to say, there is a lot of information out there on non-verbal communication, some of it very useful. With such a proliferation of 'rules' to follow, you can soon start to feel that communicating with another human is the most alien and impossible challenge imaginable. Clearly it isn't, as you've been doing it for years.

'Don't fold your arms.'
'Don't put your hands in your pockets.'
'Don't point.'
'Don't touch your face.'
'Don't lock your hands behind your back.'
'Don't lock your hands in front of your waist.'

These are just some of the rules you may have heard. However, for anyone involved in the normal give and take of daily communication, it is impossible to avoid doing some of these actions some of the time. They are totally normal after all!

The more fixated we become on these tiny gestures, the more we begin to lose sight of our instinctive ability to communicate openly.

Allow us to liberate you from these rules immediately. Please go ahead and break them. As long as you don't break the same one all the time. That's the key. Don't fold your arms *all the time*. Don't put your hands in your pockets *all the time*. Don't touch your face *all the time*.

As long as a behaviour doesn't absolutely define you, then there is no need to be hung up on it.

Rather than worrying about every move you make, there are a few simple principles you can follow to ensure you are always communicating as influentially as possible.

Just remember that these principles are designed to guide you to being fully present and communicating authentically with another person. In themselves, they are not an end; they simply prepare the path.

How to do it

Play the space

Elvis Presley was a master of non-verbal communication. Swivelling hips and a snarling lip are clearly non-verbal.

But those physical actions alone don't mean anything. Imagine your grandma doing them, and it's a very different effect. It is a mistake to imagine that by performing, or not performing, certain gestures and postures, you are necessarily communicating well.

Great performers, like Elvis or any other charismatic star, use their actions to create an atmosphere, and that atmosphere is created by the energy that the actions carry into the space they inhabit.

 The best non-verbal communicators play the space between you and them.

We've all experienced people with whom it feels impossible to have a natural, flowing conversation – these people are somehow clogging up the space between you and them.

Obviously, you probably don't want to have the impact of Elvis Presley in your office, but you do want to learn to play the space well. The trick is to change from focusing on what you are doing, to focusing on what is happening in the space between you and your colleagues.

Clear the path

Lots of things can block the path of successful communication. Picture communication flowing between people like a river; bits of detritus can dam it up if you're not careful.

This detritus can be physical: a clutter of chairs or an awkward table; permanently folded arms; a clamped jaw or furrowed brow. Or, the clutter can be psychological: emotional baggage, rigid ideas or excessive determination.

Make sure that before any communication you clear the channel to give the river a chance to flow.

1 Set the space up, move the table, organise the chairs so you can face each other openly.

2 Notice any emotional baggage you are carrying and put it down, or at least loosen your grip a little.

3 Let your arms hang loosely at your sides, breathe easily.

These simple principles will clear the path.

 The eyes have it.

Eye contact is a curious phenomenon; trivial and fleeting, yet hugely powerful and influential when playing the space between people.

Flirting begins with eye contact, setting the space between two potential love-birds alight before they've said a word. You have to be careful with eye contact to avoid the entire workforce falling in love with you or, even worse, running a mile.

The best eye contact tip going is don't be extreme, find a middle state. Excessive staring can be perceived as aggressive and intrusive.

Avoiding eye contact can be regarded as weak or evasive. The key is to develop *receptive eye contact,* which acknowledges the two-way nature of any communication. You look not only to communicate yourself, but also to receive the world and the communication of others.

Begin to regard eye contact as another place of flow between you and the world.

To stare or not to stare

People often wonder whether there is a right amount of eye contact. For how long should you hold another person's gaze?

There is no exact answer to this, other than to trust your judgement. You know immediately if someone has been making eye contact for too long; and you will have exactly the same uncomfortable feeling if you have been holding your eye contact for too long.

Keep it natural, keep it relaxed. The aim is to ensure you make contact with people; as long as your eye contact has registered and you have had a moment of recognition then that is enough. It's natural to look away to remember, consider or reflect. When you grow more confident you can play with eye contact, and practise stretching the limits of what is comfortable, but it's a risky business.

Cast your net

When trying to make eye contact with an audience of more than one, the trick is to be open and available to everyone in the room. Keep your eye contact relaxed but mobile.

- Avoid fixing on one person; avoid scanning everyone superficially.
- Make easy, open contact with everyone.
- Rather than moving from person to person in order, imagine your eye contact being cast like a net over everyone.

Use your breath

Breath balances everything. It flows both in and out, just like the best communication.

Use your breathing to support your communication. Breathe normally, breathe easily, but do breathe!

If your breath is held, then your communication will not be able to flow. If it is forced, then your communication will be forced. (See Step 4 for effective breathing techniques.)

Before you speak, breathe. It's the most important form of non-verbal communication.

Act confidently

Let your body lead your brain.

Sometimes the mind isn't helpful. It ties you in knots, floods you with worries and generally clutters up the space between you and other people.

Before you enter an important communication scenario, an interview or a pitch, it's essential to get out of your head and into your body.

Act like Usain Bolt when he has won gold: legs wide, head held high and arms stretched open like a lightning bolt (do this in private!). Imagine the lightning flowing out of your body and into the space around you and beyond.

Check out these videos from Amy Cuddy on the amazing power of posing:

www.youtube.com/watch?v=zmR2A9TnIso

www.youtube.com/watch?v=Ks-_Mh1QhMc

www.thebusinessgym.net

Your body will tell your brain to feel great!

If Usain Bolt doesn't float your boat, then choose your own example of great confidence. Choose someone who means something to you; it doesn't have to be a famous person. In fact it could even be *you* at your most confident.

Recall a time when you felt on top of the world, when you performed at your best in public. Remember how that felt, remember how you stood, walked, talked and breathed. Then carry that memory with you, like an inspiring mental photograph, and dip into the feelings it engenders whenever you need to.

If it's all going to pot

Sometimes things spiral out of control. Your nerves get the better of you and you begin to fall apart. It happens to us all. Practise this emergency routine and if you ever need it it'll be there like a reflex.

- Relax your feet into the floor – feel them soften and spread out.
- Unlock your knees – let them be soft.
- Send your body weight down through the soles of your feet.
- Let your stomach relax.
- Breathe out slowly.

Case study

A few years ago we had a jazz singer on one of our communication courses. When she was behind the microphone, singing, supported by her band, she was an expert performer. The music helped her feel confident and free in front of her crowd.

The problem arose when the music stopped, when she had to take the microphone in hand and chat between songs. Suddenly, all of her composure drained away. Without music she felt exposed, her mind flooded with unhelpful thoughts and her body clammed up. Crucially, she held her breath.

All these signals cluttered the space between her and her audience.

Without music, she was in freefall. She needed to learn to support herself, and the space between her and the paying public. By learning to let the breath flow, the eyes receive and the body lead the brain, she soon began to enjoy the vibrancy that filled the space around her and discovered new ways to support herself between songs.

 **Exercise**

Spend a day using your breath to improve the flow of communication between you and other people.

Focus on your breath throughout the day: when you get on the bus, when you're at the water cooler, when you're sitting at your desk. Without speaking to anyone, imagine the flow of breath between you and those around you.

You'll soon start to understand how communication flows, and you'll notice those people who are already receptive and those who lock you out.

Learn to let your breath lead your communication.

Call to action

- Is the space between you clear of awkward furniture?
- Are you breathing easily?
- Is your eye contact receptive?
- Is your body leading your brain?
- Can you list three people who you feel are successful communicators? Consider how they are playing the space between themselves and others.
- What do they do that creates a positive or lively atmosphere?
- How do they use the space to help people feel comfortable or excited or present?
- Is there anything that they do that you could begin to adopt?

 See effective, open body language in action:

www.thebusinessgym.net

Step 3

Maximise your voice

After reading this step you will be able to:
- Control the effect your voice has on others
- Speak with greater clarity
- Master your vocal instrument
- Self-monitor and practise effectively.

How many times have you heard a version of the much-mooted statistic: *'The words only account for 7 per cent of communication – the rest is the non-verbal'*?

This statistic is a little too precise for our liking. After all, we are talking of humans here and they are an unpredictable bunch; don't you prefer to think of yourself as an individual? The fact is, however, that no matter what the exact figures are for each individual, non-verbal is the power behind the words.

 Speaking is non-verbal . . . to an extent.

Within our spoken language is *paralanguage*. This simply means the quality of our voice and includes pitch, tone, rhythm, pace, stress and intonations.

We can choose to use these aspects of our voice to help create the desired effect but often we do not; we leave it to chance. And this is ok. The key is intention (see Step 6 on activating with the underlying verb) and if you are clear about your intention, suitably relaxed and well-practised then your communication will be clearer. The impact you have upon the listener or listeners will be the desired one.

When attempting to influence, some communications have the potential to be stressful. You may be nervous or agitated. You don't want this to show, so read on. Control your voice. Be intent and do not let your voice get the better of you!

How to do it

The lips, the teeth, the tip of the tongue

The human voice is an instrument – wind and percussive. Without becoming too technical, the breath supports the notes (the vowels) and the lips, the teeth and the tip of the tongue are the percussion section of your vocal orchestra (generally consonants). This is perhaps oversimplifying what vocal coaches would have you believe is a mystical art, but let's take the pragmatic approach.

As the receiver of spoken-word communication, the very quality and workings of that vocal orchestra have an effect on us. As the conductor of this orchestra, is it the effect you desire?

Why is it that when we hear a certain voice (perhaps the mellifluous tones of a radio presenter) it makes us want to listen on and, conversely, why do others make us want to turn off and stop listening?

 Staccato or legato?

Try this right now: Identify someone whose voice you like to listen to.

What is it about their voice that draws you in?

More than likely it's the 'legato' quality of their voice. As a musical term this means smooth and flowing. For our purposes, think of it like this:

> *The speaker has the confidence to give full length
> to the vowels sounded.*

The opposite quality to this is 'staccato'. Spiky, abrupt notes. The voice can come across as emotionally restricted, nervous, anxious and unsure of its right to be heard.

Although full of clarity and consideration, poles apart are the voices of, say, Brian Blessed (at his 'Gordon's aliiiiiive' best) or Her Majesty, the Queen. Sonorous and fluid versus clipped and giving nothing away.

Scared of singing?

Singing is the same as speaking – we just hold the notes for longer. Many people are terrified of singing in public. It is exposing. Great speakers are on the way to singing when they speak.

 **Record yourself**

Try recording yourself on your phone or computer and listen back. Often this is a horrible experience as we hear ourselves very differently every day. When we speak we hear a combination of internal and facial resonance, the acoustics of the environment (reverberation) and a version of our voice. This is not the one that others hear.

Play your voice back and listen for the quality we have just outlined. Which are you? Staccato or legato? Could you play around with more of a confident legato quality, simply by giving full weight to the vowel sounds?

When the nerves kick in, as they may well do in a pressured 'needing to influence' situation, be aware that your voice may become more clipped, more abrupt.

End of the line

Make sure that when you speak in public, you give full weight to the end of the line. Often we swallow the end words and are in danger of throwing them away, and indeed the whole message. Exude confidence by having the same energy at the end of a sentence – especially when introducing yourself or your topic in a presentation.

A smile is worth a thousand words

We can hear when someone is smiling on the phone. Smiling positively affects the resonances at our disposal and brings a brightness of tone. Record yourself again smiling and then with a face of misery – you can't help but brighten up with the smiling version and this will help create a genuine sense of calm, non-threatening influence upon the listener.

Put the brakes on

Our voices are wonderful indicators of our emotional state. Sometimes this is not a good thing! Take control. Another effect of our nerves is to speed us up, making us come across as though we want to escape, that we just want to get this conversation over and done with. Slow down. Very purposefully slow your speech down. The key to this is breath. (See Step 4 for some useful breathing exercises to help you with this.)

Pause for effect

> *'My dear Mozart, it is too exquisite for our ears; there are far too many notes in it.'*

Emperor Joseph II about *The Marriage of Figaro*

The rests are as important as the notes. Give the listener a moment to absorb. Use these pauses to maintain a calm and controlled regime of breath and thought.

And relax

Tension is exhausting; plain and simple. It can also have a negative effect on our voice. Tension affecting our posture and breathing changes our ability to support the notes and give full resonant quality. It can also be tiring and lead to serious vocal problems (just think of trainee teachers in their first term – very stressed with lots of talking). Tension in the mouth can very specifically change the effectiveness of our vocal orchestra mentioned earlier. For example, a tight and tense tongue can create an overly sibilant sound (esses) and pushing the words out causes problem plosives (Ps and Bs), which are particularly accentuated when using any kind of amplification. Record yourself again and listen out for these sounds.

So, in the same way that a piece of music can have a relaxing or invigorating effect upon us (such as Sinatra's singing style) or create tension (think *Mission Impossible*), our voices bring about an emotional response in the listener.

Rehearse, really rehearse.

If you have a key message you want to get across in an encounter, or if you are preparing for a communication to a larger audience, then rehearse.

Think of it this way. Rehearsal is never about getting it right; it's about getting it wrong, experiencing the mistakes and rectifying them before you play for real.

Speak out loud, not just vaguely running ideas in your head. Experience the language and subsequent feelings of using this language. Allow the non-verbal expression to occur congruently. Don't just think it through or plan it out on paper. Stand up and speak out loud.

Simplicity overlooked

Another effect of nerves is to limit our choice of notes, to make us sound monotonous especially when reading from a script. Is the receiver in receipt of the desired communication?

Say the following sentence out loud:

I like your red shoes.

Now emphasise each word in turn starting with 'I' on the first reading and then repeat by emphasising 'like', etc. It is so simple but we must allow our natural sense of tonality to help with meaning. The meaning of this sentence changes with every change in emphasis.

Think about this exercise when you really want to be clear on meaning – don't leave it to chance or misinterpretation.

Finally, you're excited about this new idea, this new approach or change you want to implement. Are you? Are you really? Then show it. Be excited or concerned or adamant. Connect to your emotions and appeal in real time.

Become the skilled conductor of your voice today using the exercises in this step.

Case study

Claudio had worked for a number of years as a car salesman. He was very successful and extremely confident in his ability, always over target and a prime candidate when a floor supervisor's job came up. This new supervisor's role meant giving short, inspiring talks each morning before the car-buying public descended upon the very busy forecourt.

Almost immediately Claudio lost his nerve in this new territory and it was noted by colleagues that he was just a shadow of himself when addressing the team.

This is where we came in. Claudio signed up to a public course on presentation skills that we were running in London. Throughout the day it was evident that he was entertaining, full of energy and fun and, yes, we'd have bought a car from him. In some of the exercises that involved speaking to an audience of, in this case, about eight people, he spiralled into a nervous mess. He sped up, lost clarity, fidgeted, became monotonous, lessened in personality. All in all, this vibrant and big man shrank away and looked like he wanted to escape.

During this day and in a number of coaching sessions we worked on physical grounding. Using some principles from 'actor training', Claudio was able to regain a sense of stillness, of confidence and calm. A few simple but effective vocal exercises similar to those above brought a resonant and inspiringly happy tone back. We focused on 'putting the brakes on', consciously slowing down yet driving his energy through to the end of the line. By doing so, Claudio was able to appear confident even if he didn't feel so. He put these techniques to work instantly and reported to us that his colleagues were saying, 'Whatever you've been doing, it works!'.

 Hear the impact of different vocal styles for yourself: www.thebusinessgym.net

 **Exercise**

Identify someone in the public eye whose voice you enjoy. With the knowledge above, identify and understand what qualities they have that you can aspire to.

Call to action

- Try to slow down a little and give full length to the vowels for that smooth, legato quality.
- Relax, throughout the body. Scan for where you are holding tension.
- Rehearse. Speak out loud, before doing it for real.
- Smile when you can, bring that positive tone back.
- When can you pause for effect?
- Can you think of a situation that would benefit from an improved control of voice?
- Monitor your tone and avoid the monotone. Be aware of the effect that the tone of others has on you.

Step 4

Present with power

After reading this step you will be able to:

- Appear confident
- Sound assured
- Connect with your audience
- Control your nerves and make the right impact.

Increasingly, presenting is a standard element in any job description. Whether you are a recent graduate, a middle manager or a senior leader, being able to communicate your ideas effectively and with personality to a group is an essential – and hugely influential – skill.

The trouble is, for many people there is nothing worse than having to stand up in front of a crowd and talk out loud. The fact is that presenting is one of the final tasks in the modern workplace that can leave you feeling genuinely vulnerable and exposed; where you can feel like there is no place to hide.

This step will help you stand in front of your audience with confidence, control and charisma!

 With risk comes opportunity.

When making a presentation there is a risk that you will somehow 'give yourself away' or undermine your credibility by being overcome with nerves, losing your train of thought or saying something silly.

The flip side of this risk, however, is opportunity.

Making a presentation is a rare chance to show staff, colleagues or clients what you are really made of; to let the more expressive and interesting parts of your personality run a little freer, and impress with your confidence, wit and dexterity.

The key is knowing how to do it.

 Fight or flight.

For most of us, the majority of our working life is spent sitting at a desk interacting remotely via email or the telephone, with a few face-to-face meetings or conversations thrown in for good measure. We operate well within our personal comfort zones. Presenting is very much the opposite of this standard and habitual mode of being, so when you're suddenly confronted with a live audience it can, literally, give you a fright.

The natural response to this fright is fight or flight. Or, as happens to so many, freeze up, feel awkward, say nothing and go red.

All these symptoms are a perfectly normal reaction to finding yourself in a threatening situation. The trick is being able to catch them before they dominate and to apply a few simple techniques to ensure you continue on a positive, confident-looking path.

After all, it is never truer than when presenting that 'you are your message'. If you appear terrified, the message you convey can be one of great uncertainty. However, if you appear confident, whether you are or not, the message you convey will make others confident too.

Read on to find out how to do it!

How to do it

All the best presenters (think Obama or Ant and Dec) are relaxed and easy before a crowd. This ease enables their natural personalities to flow through. For Obama, he is sincere, sensitive and empathetic, while Ant and Dec are playful, cheeky and fun.

An ounce of excess tension in any of them and all these bright, engaging qualities will dim.

 First and foremost, it is the presenter and the presenter's personality that engages an audience. The content of the presentation comes second.

Any content can be made fascinating by a lively presenter and, of course, made dull by a rigid presenter.

Given that all humans are inherently interesting, and have personalities of one kind or another, there really is no excuse for boring presentations. It is simply up to the presenter to recognise and set free their own personality and allow the audience to enjoy it.

You can be Obama, Ant and Dec or anyone in between. Just don't be dull.

Begin with the body

Relaxation begins with the body; Obama and Ant and Dec are all physically relaxed. It's not the floppy, slack relaxation of sleep, but alive relaxation – think Roger Federer in the Wimbledon final.

All the unhelpful symptoms that inhibit your presenting personality also occur in the body:

- rapid heartbeat;
- sweating;
- trembling;
- tight shoulders, chest and neck;
- short, shallow breaths;
- inability to make relaxed eye contact;
- jittery, rapid movements;
- jittery, rapid voice.

These symptoms are *normal* . . . but very unhelpful. They are also habits. The good thing about habits is that they can be broken, but it requires regular practice. This is how you do it.

When you're in the shower, at the bus stop, making a coffee, practise every day.

Finding balance

1. Stand evenly on both feet as opposed to leaning to one side.
2. Relax your feet into the floor; imagine them spreading out as if on a warm, sandy beach.
3. Send all of your body weight down through your legs and away into the floor. Let the floor support you.
4. Allow the shoulders to drop, let the top of the head float up and look straight ahead.

5. Get used to this feeling of balance, and then begin all of your presentations this way.

6. Make this a new, and better, habit!

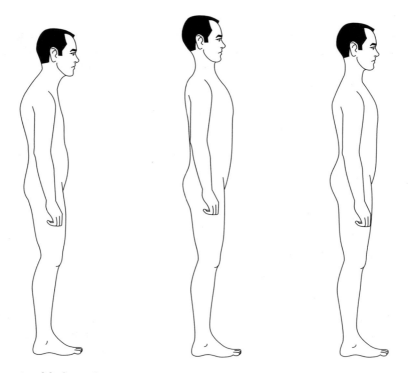

Avoid slumping or over-arching. Aim for the balanced figure on the right

Breathe to your centre

The breath is the key to remaining composed. It supports all communication. If the breath is held, then tension abounds and communication will not flow.

1. Place your thumb on your belly button and allow the palm of your hand to rest on your lower belly below it.

2. Imagine there is a balloon in your belly beneath your hand.

3. Now blow all the air out of that balloon, totally deflating it.

4. Once it is empty, simply release the pressure to allow the balloon to refill as you effortlessly breathe in.

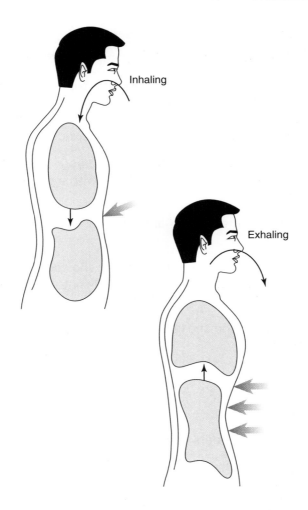

Inhaling

Exhaling

5. Do not suck the air in, just let the balloon refill. All the effort is on the out breath.

If this is hard, imagine that when you breathe in the air is flowing from the ground up through your legs and into your belly balloon. It's odd but it works!

 Check out this short video for further tips on deep breathing:

www.youtube.com/watch?v=1WMt_1jw47Q

Practise this and you will soon have a permanently centred breath.

Think tall!

Allow your head to float into the space above it.

Be aware of the space just above the top of your head, and imagine your head gently floating up into this space. Don't do anything, don't force your head up. Just imagine it floating up a little and your neck remaining free and relaxed.

Now you are creating two directions in your body: downward grounding, and a gentle upward lifting, with a centred breath in the middle.

This ensures you are open and fully occupying your personal space.

Now reach your arms out to the sides at shoulder height and feel the stretch across your chest and back. Maintain this position for a couple of full breaths before letting the arms fall.

Retain and enjoy the sense of openness and space across your upper body.

Eye contact

Look at people!

You've probably been told to 'scan the room' before? In principle, this makes sense, but only if you are actually looking at people!

Simply scanning like a robot leaves an audience cold. Get into the habit of looking at people, places and objects in a curious and engaged manner.

Look around your office – notice the floor, the ceiling, the dark corners of the room – take it all in. Notice the people in the office, their body positions, their habits, their behaviour. Engage.

Then, when in front of an audience, make sure you really engage and talk *to* them, not at them.

Case study

A senior executive from a global transport company came to us for coaching because he needed to convince the board of the company to invest many hundreds of millions of pounds in a long-term project that wouldn't turn a profit for a decade.

A tall order for anyone!

This executive was used to dealing with spreadsheets, figures and project detail, but he hadn't had to present for over five years and he was terrified.

Subsequently, he had prepared a presentation with over 200 slides, which he simply intended to read at his audience for half an hour, while he sat behind his laptop.

Alarm bells rang.

Once we'd convinced him that 'he was his message' and that he was only relying on slides to allay his anxiety, we then got to work setting him free.

We threw away the chair, and stood him evenly on both feet. However, his upper body kept shrinking in as he instinctively tried to hide, and his eyes were either glued to the floor or exploring the ceiling, avoiding his audience at all costs.

A bit more work, and he was able to stand up tall, and look at his audience.

However, he still seemed tense and couldn't be heard. We worked for three solid hours on centring his breath – it can take a while to undo unhelpful habits! Once he'd got the hang of it, though, his breath became his greatest ally, supporting him and his communication at all times throughout his talk.

As soon as he realised that he could stand in front of his audience and engage it as himself, he was set free from his script and rigid slide presentation. He no longer needed them.

 **Exercise**

The best way to practise these skills is to apply them in front of an audience. Once you have been working on them for a few days, get a few colleagues together in one room.

Allocate one person as the timer, and then take it in turns to stand in silence in front of the audience for 30 seconds.

Notice all the nervous reactions automatically occurring, and try to put your new habits into place.

If 30 seconds is easy, push it to a minute. Or 5 minutes!

Say nothing, stay silent.

Once you have mastered this complete silence with ease, then you can begin to think about what you're going to say.

This is hard, but worth it.

Call to action

- Is your body open and engaged?
- Weight evenly distributed across both feet?
- Feet relaxing into ground?
- Breath centred?
- Shoulders open and relaxed?
- Neck free?
- Can you list three presenters you admire and describe their presenting personalities?
- Can you identify four unhelpful presenting habits?
- Can you identify four helpful presenting habits?

Step **5**

Know yourself

After reading this step you will be able to:
- Define your unique positive purpose
- Identify your skills and qualities
- Stand your ground with confidence
- Let your principles guide your actions.

How many times have you heard people say:

'I'm not sure what he stands for.'

Or

'I don't know where she's heading with this.'

Or, even worse,

'There's something about him I don't trust.'

 In order to have influence, you have to stand for something.

No one will follow you if they can't feel or picture what you represent; or they sense that you are confused about your core principles.

People like clarity, and are influenced by those who offer a clear sense of purpose or meaning. This purpose doesn't have to be forceful, you don't want to be bossy or boorish; it can simply be present, resting comfortably at the heart of everything you do.

Of course, strongly held principles can be off-putting! If your guiding purpose is to win at all costs, you're soon going to wind up without many friends. It's essential that your principles and purpose are positive and can be perceived as such by others. In short, people pick up on what you stand for.

In their book *Made to Stick* (Random House, 2007), Chip and Dan Heath argue that every business has a core that guides the company's direction, and the behaviour of the staff. If the core isn't clear, or is negative, the company can lose its way. A simple example of this is Google's informal motto, 'Don't be evil!'.

Whether Google has managed to stick to this motto or not is up for debate, but this three-word statement serves as a core principle for all Google employees from graduate to board level, while clearly separating Google from images of corporate greed in the mind of the public.

The credibility of Google as a brand rests on its ability to stick to this self-proclaimed principle. And, similarly, your credibility and ability to influence rests on your ability to embody and adhere to your principles.

How to do it

Credibility

The word 'credibility' is derived from the Latin root *credo*. 'Credo' means 'I believe'; 'credibility' means the power to elicit belief in others. Hence, there is a clear connection between what you believe and the potential you have to be believed in by others.

What you believe acts as a magnetic pole on a compass, guiding both you and your stakeholders, gently pulling everyone in the same direction. The strength of the magnetic pull is entirely commensurate with the strength of your belief.

We all know the feeling of the ground giving way beneath our feet when suddenly we realise that we don't quite believe in what we are saying; and we all know that, in that instant, we have lost our audience too. People are no longer following.

The only reason this happens is that you are not, at that moment, communicating from your deepest-held beliefs, you've lost touch with your compass and been drawn into uncertain terrain.

The key to regaining your footing is to have previously identified your guiding belief and, therefore, to be able to return to it to get your bearings again. This is how you do it.

Identify your positive purpose

Just as Google has 'Don't be evil' as its core slogan, you need to distil your core to its clearest essence.

You need to define your positive purpose in the world. It is vital that your purpose is positive, that it somehow contributes to the lives of others. An entirely self-serving purpose will eventually diminish your influence and cause stakeholders to turn away.

Your purpose must also be broadly applicable. There's little point in a purpose as narrow as: 'to field customer queries within an hour'. This is a good aim, but it doesn't inform all of your communications with all stakeholders.

However, from this aim you can begin to work towards your positive purpose, which may be: 'to deepen customer understanding'.

Your positive purpose should also feel inspiring; the world of work is awash with mundane thinking, so it's essential that your purpose is magical and motivating. If it doesn't excite you, then it certainly won't excite anyone else!

Of course, your positive purpose will depend on the nature of your work. If you're a lecturer, for example, it may be: 'to transform the minds of undergraduates'. If you work in telecommunications, it may be: 'to keep people talking'.

It can be anything, as long as it's true for you and is powerful enough to guide you home.

The power to perform

Once you've identified your positive purpose in the world, the next step is to consider what gives you the power to make it happen. The ability to convert what you stand for into action is highly impressive and influential, setting apart the dreamers from the doers.

Stephen Covey, author of *The 7 Habits of Highly Effective People* (Simon & Schuster, 2004), defines a person's credibility as a mixture of their character traits and their competencies; in other words, their personal qualities and their skills. This is a great starting point, and with the addition of your positive purpose gives you a complete picture of your ability to influence.

Your power to perform your positive purpose consists of a combination of your skills and your personal qualities. All three of these facets interact to give you credibility.

Credibility = Positive purpose + Skills + Qualities

Divide a piece of paper in two. On one side list all the personal qualities that you possess that help you to function successfully; and on the other side list the hard, practical skills you have and that your colleagues rely upon you to deploy.

With your positive purpose underscoring all of these attributes, you have identified that which gives you both the right and power to influence.

Watch out for self-limiting beliefs!

Be careful not to limit your power to influence before it's even left the confines of your own brain!

So often we hear people say things like,

'I'm not really a people person.'

Or

'I'm not confident enough.'

Or

'No one will care what I think.'

While there is nothing wrong with some self-doubt – it prevents you from becoming arrogant – it is essential that you catch your mind's attempts to stymie your ability to put your positive purpose into action.

A big part of you is geared towards security, and your mind will tell you all kinds of things to make you stay still and safe. These voices are not useful when you're gathering your resources to be influential.

Pay attention when you hear your inner voices crushing your positive purpose.

Make a list of any self-limiting beliefs.

Case study

Some years ago we were called upon to coach a teacher who was failing. She'd been in teaching for a decade and for two years had received the same feedback in her observations: she left her students uninspired.

Watching in the classroom, it was clear that she had confidence. Her voice was strong, her posture assertive and her management of the children effective. However, there was no spark – something was missing.

In discussion, it transpired that over the last two years her teaching timetable had become less varied, and that she felt sidelined into teaching the least-interesting elements of her subject.

She had all the skills needed to be a good teacher, and many of the personal qualities too, but she lacked positive purpose. There was no guiding principle firing her actions, and nothing for the students to latch on to.

We worked hard on her defining her positive purpose. Initially, she offered: 'to inspire young people'.

Clearly, this wasn't working. Through being forced to examine the truth, she arrived at her real positive purpose, which was simply: 'to live as meaningfully as possible'.

This led, in the end, to her leaving teaching and setting up her own business. By reconnecting with her inner motivation, she realised the work she was doing, though noble and valid, had lost its meaning for her.

Exercise

If you're having trouble unearthing your positive purpose, a great place to start is with a personal biography and timeline.

First, draw a timeline of your life from birth until a point 10 years ahead of now.

Then mark down the key decisions you have made and events that have occurred during your life, and those you hope to happen in the next decade.

Examine what motivated your choices and notice the connections that have formed. Look for the underlying drivers at every turn, and see if you can describe each one in a sentence. Once you've recognised what has motivated you, the next step is to decide if you want to keep it or change it!

Call to action

- Can you state your positive purpose?
- Is it broadly applicable and inspiring?
- Have you identified the personal qualities and skills that set you apart?
- Are you keeping an eye on your self-limiting beliefs?
- Can you identify the positive purpose of three influential people?
- Can you think of a time when you used your skills and qualities to positively influence a situation?
- Has your positive purpose changed over your life and career?

Listen to Stephen Covey defining personal credibility:

www.youtube.com/watch?v=ACukmJ_5HSo

Step 6

Words – the emotional and logical appeal

After reading this step you will be able to:

- Plan to affect change
- Balance your appeal between the heart and mind
- Bridge the gap between your vision and the current reality.

Consider for a moment a situation in which you were influenced by a colleague or manager. Now, of course, you'll not remember the exact words used, but you will remember the effect they had on you. So, what effect did they have on you and was this just by chance?

All 'needs to influence' should begin with 'intention'. Clarity of intention. All else will follow.

If we are clear on the effect we want to effect then this will help us to decide upon the words we'll use. For over 2,000 years, since the time of Aristotle and his exploration of rhetoric, we have understood that these words must balance emotion and logic (*pathos* and *logos*).

 Intention is key.

How to do it

There are many factors that can confuse the message – noise that distorts your signal. These factors include lack of common ground, assumptions of knowledge, timing and, of course, your own emotional state, which can and will affect your delivery. Get to the very heart of your appeal and know and understand the core of your persuasion need.

Jot down a few notes right now for a potential situation in which you will need to be influential. If it helps, think of a situation that has already occurred and begin to think about how you could replay that conversation.

Think, feel, do

Whether it is to one person or an audience of 100, what do you want the audience to think, to feel and to do?

If you had only one minute, how would you get to the core? Don't think too hard – write down the words that come to mind straight away. Create a very simple script addressing what you want your audience to:

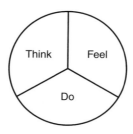

Let's look at an example:

You have pressure from the powers above to get your team to adopt a new IT system. You understand the arguments for and against. You may not even be a full-on fan of the new system, but it's going ahead whether you like it or not and your job is to encourage its use by the team.

 Using the model above, we could draft a script to encourage the team to:

Think that the department will be more efficient as a result of everyone using the new system correctly.

Feel confident that there will be support for implementation and that 'we are all in this together'.

Do take the initial steps needed to incorporate this new system into your everyday working practice.

Do comes as a result of how we think and feel.

Here is an example of think, feel, do in action:

You have a client who is considering purchasing your services. Begin by deciding what you want them to do:

Do – make a guaranteed initial booking and financial commitment; to consider working longer term with you.

To arrive at the point where the client is ready to take these actions you need to be clear on what you want them to think and feel.

Think – your service will improve their business efficiency; your service provides good value for money; you understand their specific needs.

Feel – reassured that you will deliver on all your promises; excited about the improved business efficiency.

 ## What's in your fridge?

You'll need a partner for this exercise.

1. Sit opposite each other and first simply describe the contents of your fridge.

2. Ask them what they noticed.

Usually the partner will have noticed the contents of your fridge, the specific details of how much milk and whether you're getting your five a day!

Now repeat the exercise but decide upon an intention. Use one of the following verbs to inform how you will describe your fridge to your partner:

- impress
- disgust
- educate.

Don't tell them which intention you are choosing. You certainly need to engage your imagination with this exercise; don't be afraid to be playful!

Example using impress:

> *'My fridge is made from solid platinum and the handle is diamond-encrusted. When I open the door it welcomes me with a polite salutation. Each shelf is organised into food types and starting with the bottom shelf we have a 28 Day Dry Aged Steak from our local farm. . . . '*

Allow the intention to bring about the words used.

Ask your partner to note the effect your description had upon them.

What's in your fridge? (continued)

Try it a number of times and perhaps give your partner a chance to try it too. Experiment with different intentions and see how this not only changes the effect upon the listener but also informs the words and the way in which you use them.

You can use your voice (see Step 3) to further enhance the effect.

Now think about how you could use this in a real-life situation. Clarify the intention and apply an underlying active verb to your influencing. Make a list of verbs that you could use, for example:

- praise
- encourage
- reassure.

If it helps to write a script, do try some vocal techniques (see Step 3) to bring the text to life and avoid sounding like you are just reading it.

Kirk vs Spock

Even if you've never seen an episode of *Star Trek,* you are probably aware of the difference between the characters. Kirk is all heart and emotionally connected, while the pointy-eared Spock is ruled by his Vulcan logic.

Earlier we referred to Aristotle's modes of persuasion. In a nutshell:

- **ethos** – authority/credibility – that which qualifies you to be the expert ready to appeal;
- **pathos** – the appeal to the listener's emotions;
- **logos** – the logical appeal, the facts and figures that support this.

So, assuming that you have the required ethos, let's consider the use of *pathos* and *logos*. Much as Spock's logical appeal is nearly always balanced by Kirk's passion and enthusiasm, we can approach our influencing needs in the same way.

Spoken communication relies on the emotional connection. Without it why not just email? Missing the obvious non-verbal language and effect of voice, emails and other written communication can lose a great deal of their meaning or be misconstrued entirely.

So, when speaking, balance facts and figures with emotional appeal. Consider again what you want your audience to think and to feel. Then, as a result of this, what you want them to do.

As an exercise, construct an appeal as Kirk – using only pathos. So using only feelings and emotions.

Repeat as Spock, using only logos – just list the facts and figures that you'll need to persuade. Will these ever be enough?

 Watch a short video for an example of the use of logos and pathos in a sales context:

www.thebusinessgym.net

Less certainly is more

Speak for a reason. Simple. All else is just noise.

First of all, are you asking a question or making a statement? Be clear. Really *ask* or really *state*. By doing this we avoid potential nonsense/ambiguity.

Reduce the language.

Then refine your use of language and reduce your appeal to three sentences.

Now reduce it to three words – always considering what you want your audience to think, to feel, to do? This will help you define your core/your purpose.

Concentrate the effect with less words – more words only serve to dilute the impact.

Give time to absorb and process.

Case study

Having worked with many third-sector organisations over the years, we were no strangers to coaching fundraisers on that all-important pitch that could keep the charity afloat, functioning and delivering its service for years. The clients in question, although full of passion when talking to them over coffee about the work of their organisation, relied far too heavily on facts and figures in their pitching. Where was the 'human element'? Over a few months we helped them to turn their frankly dull presentation (appealing only to the Spocks in the room) into a compelling story balancing pathos and logos. This single presentation secured funding for over two years' worth of core projects and the small charity has since adopted the approach across the board for all its pitching.

 **Exercise**

Identify the Spocks and Kirks in your working environment. What is it that defines them and the way they communicate? How successful are they and what stands in the way of their power to persuade? Now think about someone you can model your approach on, someone who balances the two characters and is close to the 'perfect communicator' you aspire to be.

Call to action

- Can you define your reason for speaking, your intention?
- Have you decided upon an active verb?
- Can you reduce the language even further to maximise impact?
- Have you balanced your appeal with pathos and logos?
- Can you think of a time when you were influenced and how pathos and logos were used effectively?

Learn more about ethos, logos and pathos in this video:

https://www.youtube.com/watch?v=_FB-ZsEaM8I

Step 7

Your audience is all that matters

After reading this step you will be able to:

- Make choices to improve perception both personally and professionally
- Motivate through conversation
- Improve awareness of your audience's position and attitudes
- Shake up existing relationships and give the desired impression.

'I suppose it is tempting, if the only tool you have is a hammer, to treat everything as if it were a nail.'

Abraham Maslow, American psychologist

Any audience, or set of stakeholders, will consist of a wide range of individuals, all of whom will respond to you in subtly different ways. There's no point in approaching each one with the same hammer, you'll only end up bending some out of shape. In this step we will help you present your best possible self to those stakeholders in order to positively influence their perception of you, and we'll consider the different ways in which your powers of influence may be having an effect.

How to do it

Perception

It is worth considering at this point just how often you have had this or a similar thought:

What do they think of me?

So what do they think of you? More importantly, what control do you have over this?

Simply put, you have no control over people's thoughts, but you can *influence* their thoughts about you.

First we'll look at improving 'you' and removing the barriers to understanding 'them'.

 Give the *real* impression.

Instead of worrying about what people think of you, spend the energy and thought on what you can do to improve your image; aim always to give a clear sense of the 'true you' in any encounter.

Because the core of much of our training comes from 'theatre practice', we have worked through every exercise and idea to make certain that at no point does a trainee or a coaching client feel like they are being made to 'pretend'. We were once asked on a public course, *'Are you suggesting that we should all be actors?'*. Not at all. What we suggest, and what underpins much of this book, is the set of skills a professional actor uses in both rehearsal and performance. Those skills of empathy, of listening, of performing, in a business scenario build foundations for success and real flexibility in communication.

 Bring yourself to your role

Identify differences between you in your *personal* life and you at *work*.

Simply score yourself 1–10 when answering these questions. For example, if you are very flexible in your personal life then you could score high (an 8 or 9?).

	Personal	Work
How easy do you find it to say 'no'?		
How relaxed do you feel when communicating a new idea?		
To what extent do you feel that your words carry weight?		
How willing are you to listen to others and adapt your plans?		
How confident are you in a new social encounter?		

Notice any disparity – identify where you could score higher in the work environment.

Why do these differences occur? Is there a way of letting a little more of *you* out at work to give that 'real' impression – can you let your guard down a little?

A colleague was going through the breakdown of a major personal relationship. People at work knew there was something amiss and in this difficult time she let them in a little. Previously she had 'played' the role of an impervious, strict, hard taskmaster – really trying to maintain the impression of 'boss'. After this period she said that actually her work relationships dramatically improved because they saw her as human and fallible, and she in turn was able to drop her guard and became far more approachable as a result.

Now, you don't need to go through a personal trauma for this to work but, as in the example above, think about dropping your guard and allowing others to see more of the real you.

In the next step (Communicate well) we'll work through some ways to make your communication more meaningful and suggest methods to create and develop that all-important rapport.

Water-cooler moments: getting to know you

Create opportunities for conversation. Be the person that makes time for people, no matter how busy you are. As influencing is 'long term', invest in relationships.

We should remember not to overlook the value of small talk. In Britain we are obsessed with the weather! When we talk about the weather to someone we don't know very well we are checking their 'agreeability'. Much like in the animal kingdom (think dogs sniffing each other or monkeys grooming), we start with simple small talk and gradually build trust.

After all, small talk can help lay the path to big talk. Once an improved sense of understanding, of agreeability and of position is settled upon you can move on to the 'influencing need'.

Also, we mentioned how smiling can affect the voice in such a positive way in Step 3:

> **'Wear a smile and have friends; wear a scowl and have wrinkles.'**
>
> George Eliot, author

Do this now. Write a list of your important relationships at work (you could use the examples you identified in Step 1). Plan for conversational opportunities – not falsely setting them up but preparing yourself to be ready to have a chat when the next opportunity arises.

You may have got off on the wrong foot with someone. You may have experienced difficult encounters with others. Gradually reshape these relationships. Drip-feed the changes in you and your approach to avoid any *'Who is this person?'* – type thoughts from others.

If you are starting off in a new role or even better in a new place of work, you could take this opportunity to re-invent yourself. But stick with the genuine; allow a little more of the real you to surface.

Going forward, jargon free

Do this now. Avoid 'fad' language. Superfluous language choices such as 'going forward' are just that – superfluous! Be wary of the overuse of organisation- or industry-specific phrases and acronyms as your wider circle of stakeholders may be clueless. They may not tell you that they don't understand, leaving *you* clueless as you undermine your message.

Although, of course, acronyms can be useful, surely the point is to help with language and not add to confusion. If you are using acronyms at work, can you be certain that everyone knows what you are talking about? They are useful for written language but when spoken, be careful.

Acronym checker

Which acronym is three times longer than the original words when spoken? The answer is one that we all know and use: 'www' becomes 'double u double u double u' – yes, this really takes three times as long to say as 'world wide web'. This is now a universal standard, but in a business context see if you can spot others that you and your colleagues use!

Assumptions

Before approaching with your 'influencing need' – what do you think you know about your audience? Assumptions can be a barrier to understanding.

Along with the assumption of understanding of acronyms or industry-specific language, can you think of any other assumptions you make when communicating?

We can often make assumptions:

- of knowledge;
- of understanding;
- of interest.

Maybe you have been warned about the personality of the person you are aiming to influence? Maybe you have had a difficult past encounter?

Be brave and throw assumptions out. Challenge yourself to start each chapter of communication afresh. As you make assumptions, so does the other person.

Use each communication to build a picture of the individual that will help you in tailoring your approach in a useful way. Refer to the model in Step 6 and sense if your target is more Spock than Kirk. Listen, evaluate and adapt your approach; at all times make it a conversation, allowing more of your true self to come through, and validate the other person through powerful listening.

Finally, speak logically and with emotion.

 Watch a short animation to find out how your assumptions may be holding you back:

www.thebusinessgym.net

Case study

We were contacted by an organisation that had a relatively new, young member of staff. The problem, as management saw it, was that this young man did not 'gel' well with others; he made little effort to socialise within the workplace. Managers felt that they did not know him well enough to trust him with all-important face-to-face contact with their high-level clients. His role demanded this and they expressed little faith in his ability to communicate effectively. They had addressed the issues in appraisals and sent him on a few courses in the hope that he would 'up his game', as they put it.

We met him. Our first impression was that this charming, polite and very well-mannered young man felt intimidated by many of the staff in his office, most of whom had years of experience in their industry. Yes, he struggled daily with the communication part of his role and his confidence had eroded over the almost-12 months he had been there. In our sessions we drew out just how different he was in his personal social life. He was exuberant and stated that his friends would not recognise the version of him that he played at work.

Over a couple of months, he allowed himself to have those 'water-cooler moments' and build relationships at work. Other employees felt that they had started to get to know him and trust grew mutually. He, in turn, felt more confident and went on to real success within the organisation.

(Incidentally, the staff with whom we met were acronym-heavy and loved their jargon . . . while he was free of this.)

 **Exercise**

Reflect upon a difficult working relationship. Try to list a few ways that you could have improved this relationship. No matter how difficult they were, in your opinion, identify a change in approach. Could the relationship have benefited simply from throwing out some of the assumptions you had made? Now think about what steps you could take to reshape and improve, not just this but all of your work encounters.

Call to action

- Can you identify the differences in your personality when at work and at home?

- Have you considered how you can improve your image?
- Can you make your language almost jargon free?
- Are you standing tall and confident?
- Are you ready to show you are flexible and allow yourself to be influenced?

Step **8**

Communicate well

After reading this step you will be able to:
- Listen with depth
- Balance your internal and external experiences
- Be fully present
- Improvise and communicate flexibly.

Successful relationships depend on meaningful communication; but how do we know we are communicating meaningfully?

We certainly know when someone is communicating with us in a meaning*less* way. We've all been trapped listening as someone talks relentlessly, without pause for breath. From their point of view, they're in full meaningful flow, every word they say is awash with value and insight. But you have lost interest, their monologue is nothing but a stream of noise. You begin to feel bored, agitated and even angry. In effect, what they are saying has become meaningless.

We all construct our own meaning; however, successful communication requires that our personal meanings are shared with and changed by others in order to create something new.

 Communication, at its best, is a creative act between two or more people.

It is a grave mistake to assume that presenting your personal meaning is enough to engender this shared meaning.

The previous step focused on honing your impact and ensuring that the signals you send are the signals you wish others to receive. This step requires you to turn your broadcast speakers off and switch your receptive microphones on.

Creating meaning with others begins by allowing them space to flourish, and then tuning in to find the places where you connect.

How to do it

Make space

Communication happens in the space between two people; the way you affect that space determines how well the communication is likely to go. The key is to keep the space between you uncluttered, flexible and alive.

The first step to creating an open space is to be aware of yourself: of the emotional baggage you carry into a conversation, of how rigidly you are projecting your ideas, of the attitudes you hold towards others. With this awareness, you automatically begin to create space around these ideas, emotions and attitudes; this space, in turn, makes you available to others.

On this foundation of self-awareness it is possible, with a few guiding ideas, to build sensitive and meaningful communication with almost anyone.

Shut up and listen!

'Active listening' have become buzz words in recent years, with many people trained to believe that by performing certain 'listening skills', such as smiling, nodding, making constant eye contact, saying 'Mmm' and physically mirroring their partner, they are listening successfully. The trouble is, amid this flurry of 'listening behaviours', people often forget to listen.

The key to good listening is to listen. Stop speaking, stop offering opinion, stop making suggestions, stop offering solutions, stop judging, stop everything and listen.

 Listen with a desire to understand your partner.

As the author Steven Covey said, 'Seek first to understand.' Only once you have acquired some degree of understanding can your communication be meaningful.

The 'active listening' behaviours are useful in that they direct you towards your partner, as opposed to towards yourself, but all that really matters is that you listen with an absolute desire to hear and understand.

 Try this with a partner:

1. Ask them to tell you about a favourite holiday.
2. Give them 100 per cent of your listening focus.
3. After a while reduce your focus to 50 per cent, and finally cut it to 5 per cent.
4. Then swap roles and let your partner get revenge.

The power of real listening will soon become abundantly clear!

 Check out the impact of genuine listening:

www.thebusinessgym.net

Balance the internal and external and be present

Presence is a constant interplay between your external experience and your internal world, and the Dalai Lama embodies this gentle, subtle skill. He observes his inner realm, and the responses it produces to his environment, and interacts with others by observing them, listening to them and allowing his inner world to blend with theirs.

The Dalai Lama is aware of both the external and the internal at all times, making him as available to the present moment as it is possible to be, and enabling him to fully *be* with others.

Clearly, he's had a lot of practice!

 See the beautiful, easy presence of the Dalai Lama:

www.youtube.com/watch?v=vXS-PIKLoSU

But if you cut off from either your own inner sensations, feelings or thoughts, or from the external reality of others, you snap out of full presence. The primary technique of great communicators is their ability to tread the fine line between their inner world and external experience.

 Listen to acclaimed voice teacher Patsy Rodenburg talk about the power of presence:

www.youtube.com/watch?v=Ub27yeXKUTY

Try a little meditation to help you tune into your subtle presence.

1. Sit comfortably in a chair, feet flat on the floor, back straight, hands resting in your lap.

2. Close your eyes and slowly breathe in and out. Listen to your breath. Take 10 long, slow breaths. Allow the out-breath to lengthen.

3. Then, breathing softly, allow your attention to drift to the sounds you can hear in the room, and the outside world beyond. Spend five long breaths listening to the sounds.

4. Next, open your eyes and allow the visual experience of the room back in, again taking five long breaths to do this.

5. Finally, relax, breathe normally and stay present with all the sensations you have just experienced, allowing them to sit in your awareness without effort.

Practise this and you'll begin to carry greater presence and awareness into all your communication.

In his influential book, *Flow*, Mihály Csíkszentmihályi described good communication as an 'autotelic' activity. An autotelic activity is an activity that is performed only for the satisfaction it gives; it is not a route to a predetermined goal – it is an end in itself. When you're communicating in this way, time flies and people enjoy themselves.

True presence brings people into pleasure.

Empathy

Empathy builds bridges between people, and frequently follows good listening and full presence. Without empathy there can be no collaboration.

As a listener, it is important to empathise with both your partner's thoughts and with their feelings.

A very simple technique for ensuring that there is empathic understanding is to listen, summarise and check.

 Try this:

1. Let your partner explain their point of view. Listen.

2. Then summarise it in your own words as best you can.

3. Next, crucially, ask them: is that about right? Are there any changes you'd like me to make?

4. Then, listen again. By doing this you allow your partner to guide your understanding of them.

 Check out this video of the amazing Daniel Goleman on the power of presence and empathy:

https://www.youtube.com/watch?v=HTfYv3IEOqM

Improvise

By now you'll be in full connection with your partner, so it's time to start building ideas. The best improvisers build ideas together easily – think of great sports teams or musicians playing together, all following each other's lead, all picking up on each other's signals, all working to create something new and immediate.

This can be carried into communication by following one simple principle: accept and build.

Accept any idea from anyone and build upon it. Say 'yes' to them, and offer something of your own in return.

If, in a meeting, you realise you've said no to everything anyone has offered, try a change of tack and say yes! This doesn't mean you've agreed to it, it simply means you've heard it and are willing to run with it and see where it leads.

Be careful, it's very easy to overuse the phrase 'Yes, but . . .', which is a way of gently closing down someone's idea. It's possibly a habit to break. The phrase 'Yes, and . . .' is very useful. Begin your response to an idea with 'Yes, and. . .'. You'll soon start opening doors you never knew existed.

 Here's Karen Tilstra at TED on the power of saying 'Yes, and . . . ':

http://youtu.be/l1SK_qNLx5U

Take your aim

Of course, in a business setting all parties usually have an agenda; rarely is communication aimless.

Make sure you know your aim before you begin communicating. Set your target: for example, 'to secure a new client'.

Your aim will guide you through the conversation, giving you something to head towards at all times. Of course, you must be flexible here. Your aim is only a part of the conversation, it isn't the dominating feature.

You may not achieve your aim at the first attempt, but over time you will gradually ease closer to it.

Consider carefully how you to communicate your aim. On some occasions it may be advantageous to state your desire loud and clear up front: for example, 'I'd like to see us working together for many years to come.'

Some people love the bold approach. However, in other circumstances you may decide to keep your aim as something underlying a softer set of tactics. An aim can be stated midway into a meeting or even tacitly understood without needing to be declared.

The key is to consider a tailored approach for every stakeholder. Always ask yourself: 'What will work best for them?'.

Case study

A new employee in the marketing department of an NHS trust was having difficulty fitting in with her new colleagues; they couldn't see eye to eye on anything.

In our sessions together, it was revealed that she'd joined the department straight after leaving a highly pressured position in news journalism. She was used to competing hard and looking after her own interests to get her story on the front page. She kept information secret and protected her ideas.

Her new colleagues found her rude and abrasive.

Simply by switching her focus to listening and seeking to understand the needs of others, we enabled her to let go of the tight, defensive grip she held on her feelings and thoughts and, gradually, she settled into presence with her colleagues. We then extended this presence with the principle of 'accept and build', and soon she and her colleagues were creating linked chains of fresh ideas together. They were collaborating, both emotionally and intellectually.

 **Exercise**

Hone your improvisational skills by playing 'Yes, and . . . ' with a partner.

1. Together you're planning a trip abroad. To every suggestion your partner makes you must say 'Yes, and . . . ' and then make a suggestion of your own.

2. Your partner then, in turn, responds with 'Yes, and . . . ' and a suggestion of their own.

Try to pick up on your partner's offer and make a suggestion that naturally follows, rather than coming up with a totally new idea.

The better you get at playing 'Yes, and . . . ', the better you'll be at building collaborative ideas.

 Here's an explanation of how to play the 'Yes, and . . . ' game:

https://www.youtube.com/watch?v=cSzCfsGvwj0

Call to action

- Are you listening with a desire to understand?
- Are you attending to your partner's thoughts and feelings?
- Are you present with your inner feelings and external experience?
- Are you using 'Yes, and . . . ' to build ideas with others?

Step 9

Be authentic, be concise

After reading this step you will be able to:
- Tell your story
- Deliver a meaningful personal pitch
- Communicate authentically
- Get to the point when you need to.

The ability to communicate authentically and quickly is an essential influencing tool – sometimes you simply need to get to the point by the shortest possible route.

Your ability to be concise and direct is tightly intertwined with your level of authenticity. The moment someone starts to waffle is often the moment they have lost contact with their authentic message.

 As an influential communicator, you need to have both a personally meaningful message and the skill to deliver it with aplomb. One without the other is virtually useless.

Being concise in itself is irrelevant unless what you say retains a direct connection to your deeper story and purpose. It is easy, when under pressure, to respond with a sharp, but ill-considered remark that, ultimately, may come back to haunt you.

In order to create authentic, concise communication you need to hone your message: like a sculptor with a shapeless lump of marble, you chisel and chip away until all that remains is the essential form within.

Let's get to work with your lump of marble and start giving it some shape.

How to do it

 What is authenticity?

Imagine there are two cowboys, both in the same cowboy garb, both astride a horse. Only one is a real cowboy, the other is an actor in a cowboy costume.

How would you know the difference between the real and the fake?

From looking at them, assuming they both had rugged features and weather-beaten complexions, there would be no way of telling them apart. They'd both look like cowboys.

And, in business, most people look like real business people. They present themselves in the appropriate costume. They appear authentic.

Next, you could ask the cowboys to tell you about themselves. At this stage, if he hasn't constructed a passable cowboy biography, the fake may be revealed. However, he may still be as convincing as the real cowboy. If this is the case, further interrogation would be required.

Eventually, the identity of the fictional cowboy would become apparent when, perhaps, he failed to answer more nuanced or subtle questions about life in the Wild West as easily as the real cowboy. You'd also, probably, notice signs of greater physical stress as the pressure increased on his fabrication.

However, the real cowboy would retain an effortless connection to his own biography and life experience. He'd be speaking from his authentic self as there'd be no need for him to do otherwise, and this authentic self would emanate from every pore of his being.

 Your story, _your_ lived experience, _your_ life is the source of _your_ authenticity. Authenticity is personal; you can only be yourself.

Only by communicating from this source can you remain relaxed and genuine in all circumstances.

 Write the story of your skills

- Complete the personal biography exercise at the end of Step 5.
- Identify five key strengths, they can be skills or qualities, which you believe define you in the workplace. For example, you may be a deep thinker, or an expert at managing complex systems, or perhaps you have a flair for design.
- For each strength, locate the point in your biography where that skill or quality began to develop or was first demonstrated.
- Expand your biography at that point, detailing how the particular strength was discovered and explored. Fill in as much specific detail as possible; really paint the picture.
- Trace the journey of that strength through your biography. Note any key events that have developed or informed the progress of that strength.
- Make sure you articulate how the strength has changed and grown over time, until you arrive at your present position.
- Repeat this for all of the strengths you identified.

Through this exercise you begin to recognise your core skills as an embedded and authentic part of your life story. They are not a superficial add-on.

This unification of your biography and your skill set provides the perfect pallet for authentic, confident communication.

Build your personal brand

Along with the positive purpose you identified in Step 5, this bigger-picture story of your unique personal skill set and qualities gives you a constant resource to remain anchored in. It provides you with a piece of unshifting solid ground to stand upon.

Now it's time to reduce and shape your language even further by creating your **personal brand.**

1. Write your name in the middle of a piece of paper.

2. Below it write your positive purpose: e.g. 'David – to help people communicate.'

3. Below this write three questions: **Why? What? How?**

4. Underneath **why**, in one sentence, write why you hold your positive purpose: e.g. 'In order to reduce the amount of confusion and frustration in the world.'

5. Underneath **what**, write down what you do that makes your positive purpose occur: e.g. 'I work with staff in businesses and similar organisations, either as a trainer or a coach, to deepen their understanding of communication.'

6. Underneath **how**, write down the methods you use to fulfil your positive purpose or the beliefs that inform them: e.g. 'I use empathy to understand my clients, and am then able to provide them with the techniques they need to develop.'

7. Now practise speaking these aloud in turn, as if you're introducing yourself to somebody new: e.g. 'Hello, I'm David, and I help people communicate more effectively in order to make work less frustrating.'

Or:

'Hello, I'm David and I help people communicate by providing training in influencing skills.'

 Define your personal brand right now with the help of a video:

www.thebusinessgym.net

Check out this video for a great example of a similar exercise with a well-known brand:

https://www.youtube.com/watch?v=phyU2BThK4Q

The one-word challenge

Once you've streamlined your personal brand to three key sentences, the next and toughest challenge is to reduce it to one indestructible, atomic word. A word that encapsulates your ultimate quality, skill or purpose in the world.

For example: 'David – Communication.'

On the back of your sheet of paper, write as many words as you can in one minute that sum up your personal brand.

Then spend another minute crossing out all the words that are even slightly peripheral, until you are left with only a handful.

Be as brutal as you can, until there is only one word left. This word is your touchstone. This word rests at the heart of everything you do.

 Check out author Daniel Pink on pitching:

https://www.youtube.com/watch?v=XvxtC60V6kc

Be as meaningful as possible

Those who make what they say most meaningful are those who have the greatest impact.

The way to stay meaningful is both to remain continually connected to the bigger picture and to ensure your audience remains connected to the same big picture.

When presenting or pitching any idea, always begin with the bigger picture.

- **Make sure you tell your audience the context** – the ice caps are melting as a result of global warming, which is caused by the burning of fossil fuels. This is creating devastating flooding across Europe.

- **Then go on to describe your idea** – if everyone pledges to walk to work on a Friday and leave their car at home. . . .
- **Then tell them the result of that idea** – then the UK's carbon emissions would be cut by a quarter.
- **Finally, and vitally, reconnect this to the bigger picture: tell them what it means** – this would slow the rate of global warming by 2 per cent, ensuring the ice caps thaw more gradually, which in turn would reduce flooding in Northern Europe, saving millions of people from misery.

 Always begin with the context and end with the meaning.

Case study

A charity client came to us with a need to prepare a major pitch for a potentially transformative investor. If it secured investment, then its campaign work would be financially viable for the next five years, but it was up against two rival charities.

The charity was to have an hour to pitch its cause to the investor before he flew back to America.

We worked hard on making the story memorable, meaningful and compelling. We created the perfect script and slide deck. We also trained the presenters to ensure they were confident in their delivery.

Luckily, on our final afternoon of preparation, we asked each presenter (there were three) to create a three-sentence pitch and a single-word brand for both themselves and the presentation.

On the day itself, the first two rival organisations overran and, as the investor had to catch a flight, this left only 15 minutes for our team to convince him. As a result of the message-reduction work, they were able to adjust their delivery, focus on the essentials and convey the core message succinctly. This, in turn, showed the investor that they were skilled communicators with great personal conviction. He was assured that his funds would be wisely used.

Needless to say, our client won the investment!

 **Exercise**

A great way to prepare for a presentation, once you've written it, is to reduce it.

Just as with your personal brand – first, write the complete biography of the presentation. When did the idea of it first emerge? Why was it exciting? What journey has it been through?

Then, define the unique positive purpose of the presentation.

Then use **Why? What? How?** to create three definitive sentences that encapsulate the presentation's message.

And, finally, reduce your presentation to a single word.

Once you've completely stripped your presentation to its essentials, you'll be in full command of its meaning and you'll feel confident fielding questions.

Call to action

- Are you working from your authentic life story?
- Can you communicate your essence in three sentences?
- Have you identified your single-word brand?
- Is everything you say connected to the bigger picture?

Step **10**

Play the long game

After reading this step you will be able to:

- Identify your allies
- Build trust
- Set your long-term goals
- Plan your influencing strategy over the next five years.

The circle is complete: we're back with relationships.

All the best relationships develop and change over time; in fact, unless a relationship develops and changes it usually breaks down and, as we know, if the relationship breaks down, you lose your power to influence.

 Maintaining meaningful relationships is essential to ensure you retain the ability to influence; the longer you stay in a relationship with someone, the greater your influence becomes.

This is true whether the person is a client, colleague, service provider, employee or friend. The more both parties feel they know and trust each other the more they are able to sway each other's thinking. Relationships without trust tend to lead to negative influence, with neither party willing to follow the other's lead or listen to their ideas.

The key is to build trusting, long-lasting relationships. This is where everything we have discussed in the previous nine steps comes into play: the sole purpose of every tip, technique and exercise in this book is to enable you to build mutually beneficial, meaningful relationships with a diverse range of stakeholders.

It's important not to be too tactical and calculating, as overly engineering relationships rarely works; it's enough to have one eye on the long term and to know that every honest interaction you have with someone, no matter how fleeting, builds the connection between you.

How to do it

Be interested and flexible

Take an interest in your stakeholder's world. This sounds so obvious, but it is very easy to lose sight of the broader picture of a person and reduce them to a business transaction, especially if they're not, in that particular moment, giving you what you need.

All relationships ebb and flow, they are an ongoing process, so when things feel stuck between you, it's your wider interest in them and your ability to empathise with them that will get the wheels in motion again. A little bit of deeper interest in your stakeholder soon oils the cogs.

In order to allow the relationship to flow again you also need to be flexible; to remember that what you need from that client or colleague in that particular moment isn't the full picture. It's amazing what can happen if you let your focus broaden a little, and allow your stakeholder to find their own way towards meeting your needs. By showing flexibility you give your stakeholder the room they need to manoeuvre, which in turn helps them to trust you.

Show willing

Be willing to listen, communicate and share your knowledge and expertise whenever you can. Be generous; don't hold back.

Frequently, we withhold information or fail to use our skills because we feel uncertain, nervous or protective. Be brave, speak up. If you don't, people may never know you can.

Through being prepared to make an offer, you enable others to feel comfortable in making an offer too and, once again, you build trust with those around you.

Communicate honestly

Share as much of the information you have as and when you can. Again, it's honesty that counts here. There's nothing more off-putting than someone evading the question, or deliberately skirting the edges of an issue.

Be honest. Even if this honesty demands that you say 'I'm sorry I can't share that with you right now, but I will as soon as I can.' Or, 'I can't give you a clear answer yet, because we haven't decided.'

Honesty doesn't have to know the answer, it can embrace uncertainty too. If you communicate your full position authentically, with delicate sensitivity to the impact your position may have on others, then, over time, you gain the trust of colleagues and clients alike.

Be meaningful

Unless someone understands your reasons for behaving in a certain way then, to them, your actions can appear meaningless.

Put people in the picture; never assume that, just because something makes sense to you, it makes sense to them.

We've all been told to do something at work with no explanation as to why, resulting in a half-hearted engagement with the task. Humans thrive on meaning; if something makes sense we give it all we've got.

It pays to take a little extra time to put things in a meaningful framework.

Take responsibility

When the going gets tough, the tough get going. Or at least they take responsibility for what needs to be done.

When communication is at its most fraught, when bad news needs to be delivered or when someone's feelings are at stake, it's essential to engage fully.

At moments like that, email or text is not the way. By meeting face to face or, failing that, on the telephone, you are able to communicate more fully, delivering difficult messages with all the compassion and sensitivity you can.

Part of being influential long term is learning to recognise the moments when you need to step into the fire, feel the heat of a situation and dowse it by being fully physically present. It's tough, but fills people with respect for you.

Case study

You never know at the start where a relationship might carry you. Every small beginning has the potential to lead to rich and varied opportunities.

Some years ago we ran a presentation skills course at a blue-chip consulting company. Ed, one of the delegates on the course, was a newly recruited recent graduate in his first year of work. His junior post in the HR department meant that he spent a lot of time fielding emails and helping to organise more senior staff members' diaries.

On the day of the course we got on well and chatted about shared interests outside of work, and at the end of the day we gave Ed an extra half an hour of one-to-one coaching and agreed to connect on LinkedIn.

Two years later, we received an email from Ed, who by now had finished his graduate role and was working in the training team of a large bank. He asked if we still delivered presentation skills training as his new team needed to brush up their skills. Again we delivered the training, chatted to Ed at length and agreed to meet for coffee to talk about some of the communication issues he was having in his new role.

Now over five years since our first meeting with him, Ed has become the training manager at the bank and regularly calls us for a quick catch up and to find out if we can help him with a communication skills issue. It's a mutually beneficial, trusting, long-term relationship.

 **Exercise**

Start building alliances early.

Take a moment or two to think back over all the people you have met through work over the past six months, some of whom you may not have spoken to since, others you may interact with occasionally and some, perhaps, you speak to often.

Focus on those people whom you found interesting in some way – whether it was their job, their demeanour or what they had to say – but haven't seen much of since you first met them.

These relationships are like seeds lying in untended ground. They won't grow.

Start tending to them today.

You've already made a start by bringing them into focus. Now seek opportunities to connect, find out what they're up to and stay in touch.

Call to action

- Do you take every opportunity to share your skills and expertise?
- Do you always take the time to frame your communication with meaning?
- Are you nurturing any long-term relationships?
- Do you take responsibility for tricky communication?
- Can you name the practical steps you will be taking over the year to nurture new and potentially lasting relationships?

Part 2

10 influencing skills in action

This and the next part of this book will guide you through many common influencing situations, helping you apply the skills and ideas from this book in real life. Before you read these sections we'd like to remind you of the three principles for successful influence we offered in our introduction:

1. Prepare yourself
2. Maintain relationships
3. Communicate clearly.

These principles provide a simple checklist, which will help you identify any weak spots in your ability to influence.

Are you prepared?
Is there a relationship?
Are you communicating well?

No matter whom you are trying to influence, answering these three simple questions will give you an immediate insight into how you can improve.

Influencing a team

Are you prepared?

'O Divine Master, grant that I may not seek to be consoled, as to console. To be understood, as to understand.'

Saint Francis of Assisi

Surely a 13th-century forerunner to Stephen R. Covey's *'Seek first to understand . . . '*?

No matter who thought of this maxim for communication, we can and should use it here. To truly be part of and be seen to be a useful functioning member of any team, you need to focus on understanding the individuals.

Where are you in the sphere?

Begin by referring back to Step 1 and carry out a relationship audit of the team. Map out the relationships as described and use this to hone in on those that need strengthening. Work through the exercise and actually put pencil to paper to identify the areas of imbalance.

Aim for relationships that are balanced in terms of their influence on you and yours on them. An imbalance in either direction will surely topple as one of you is going to feel powerless, leading to disengagement.

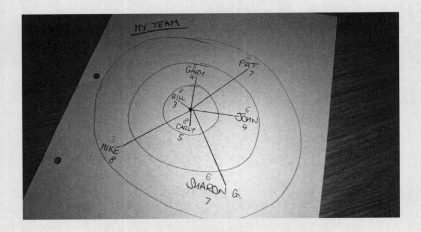

Then, and only then, can you increase your 'gravitational effect' on the team as a whole.

Consider the reasons as to why there is an imbalance. Have you spent enough time and energy working on these relationships? Have you travelled the easy path and spent that time and energy on the relationships that come easy, feel natural and are thought of as friendships?

Re-route right now and spend a greater portion of that time and energy on the difficult/challenging relationships.

What can you learn from previous team meetings/ experiences?

You may want to keep a notebook of those relationships that you have identified as needing work. Note what:

- interests team members;
- motivates them;
- annoys them;
- bores them;
- excites them, etc.

Consider how you can tap into these notes when communicating with them. Through this approach they will hopefully start to feel that you are 'understanding' them and therefore you are building the relationship – the sense of mutual trust and influencing becomes easier and collaborative.

Can you define your positive purpose?

Look over Step 5. Don't expect others to really know you and what you stand for unless it trips off the tongue for you. This modern-day elevator pitch and the understanding of how it motivates you should underpin your communication at all times, with transparency.

Can you also apply this to your team as a whole? Perhaps there is an exercise in working with your team to agree on the nature of this. How and why does it contribute to the success of the organisation as a whole? Next time you book an away day with this team, if you haven't done so already see if you can set aside some time to define the team's positive purpose.

Mitigating any confusion over the collective purpose in this way is a sure-fire method of improving workflow and overall productivity. We aim for shared ownership of ideas, process and success.

Is there a relationship?

Well, yes, there are many: relationships with individuals that make up the team and the relationship with the team itself.

Make the most of encounters with members of the team. Create opportunities to find out more about them, how they like to communicate.

In one-to-one encounters, cultivate a trusting relationship in which you show genuine interest (refer again to Step 1).

With those in your outer orbit, make that journey, attend that face-to-face meeting. Really try *not* to cancel on them; make them a priority. Be interested and be flexible. As you come to understand each other, that interest in each other's position and the flexibility of the position can only serve to get you on the same page – or at least in the same chapter!

If the encounters are fleeting, make the most of them. Be authentic, be concise. Consider how you can streamline your communication with them. Choose your underlying active verb to be *kindle* (ignite the relationship or idea), *excite* (about the relationship and what you can achieve together) or perhaps *intrigue* (arouse their curiosity).

In team meetings or conference calls, or indeed presentations, it's likely that no one will thank you for running over time. At this point it's worth remembering the law of diminishing returns.

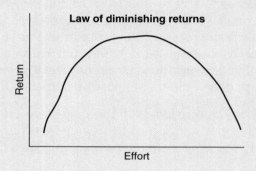

As you add words and reiterations in your communications, not only do they decrease in value but you run the risk of negative returns – undermining all that has gone before. Be authentic, be concise.

Alliance building

Looking back at the universe of influence you drew, can you take a piggyback ride (Step 1)?

Analyse your atmosphere and inner orbit and see if someone with whom you have a stronger relationship exerts a greater gravitational force on someone you originally placed in your outer orbit.

Develop an alliance with those closer to you and aim to draw in those currently drifting in the outer orbit.

Are you communicating well?

Are you stuck in a communications rut because of your:

- self-limiting beliefs;
- stubbornness;
- 'we've always done it this way' response pattern;
- thinking that to *be influenced* makes you weak.

Break these now, especially the one about thinking that to allow yourself to 'be influenced' is weak. It's not at all – in fact, you have the power to choose to allow this influence to occur.

Think of a situation where you could have allowed yourself to be influenced to change your mind, to follow a different practice or simply to try something new. Ask yourself why you will not allow yourself to be influenced. Do you consider it to be a weakness? Do you worry that others will perceive it in this way? Of course to allow yourself to be coerced, manipulated or tricked into something or a way of thinking is not ideal. Coercion, manipulation and trickery are negative and they can make you feel silly, used, weak or powerless.

Positive forms of influence, such as inspiration, require you to drop your guard. Allow yourself to be positively influenced and to be seen to be. Consider and choose – you have the power.

Quid pro quo

A further benefit of 'allowing yourself' to be influenced by members of your team is the trust it can help to build. You will be seen as flexible, approachable and a team player.

In no particular order, see if you can tick these off:

- Aim to understand differences/preferences.
- Deal with individuals – not the team.
- Start with *listening* – make certain that you build those strong relationships by listening.
- Be able to list the priorities of each team member – seek out what is important to them.
- Be *clear* about what you want and keep an open mind.
- They need to understand what works for you – and vice versa. Is this the case?
- Empathise. Summarise thoughts and feelings to show you understand. Allow yourself to be influenced.

These days many of us work remotely, which can bring benefits to businesses and their employees. However it is important to remember that there's simply no real substitute for face-to-face interaction.

> **'The human moment has two prerequisites: people's physical presence and their emotional and intellectual attention.'**
>
> Edward M. Hallowell (psychiatrist), *The Harvard Business Review,*
> January 1999

Skill 2

Influencing a colleague

Is there a relationship?

When wishing to have a particular influence upon a colleague it is essential, first, to understand the nature of your relationship with them.

There are many different types of colleagues and each brings their own set of specific traits in relation to you. Picture your current work colleagues for a moment and you'll immediately realise that you relate to each one differently, no matter how subtle the difference.

At work we are always inhabiting both our professional self and the more relaxed self we are naturally outside of work. Often, the more senior the colleague, the more of our professional self we tend to inhabit around them. The more equal a colleague, the more comfortable we feel to be our natural self around them. Of course, there are also senior colleagues with whom we feel very comfortable, and equal colleagues with whom we have no relationship but the professional.

The interaction of these two roles, professional and personal, is an important element in your influencing style with each colleague.

Consider your colleagues again and note the nature of the relationship with each. Does it tend to the professional or the personal?

The key is to find a balance of the two with each colleague. It doesn't need to be an even balance but, for example, if you have an entirely professional relationship with someone it will be beneficial to infuse it with a bit of your personal qualities, and vice versa.

Professional influence

- Organised
- Punctual
- Thorough
- Expert
- Effective

Personal influence

- Humour
- Interest/curiosity
- Friendliness
- Warmth
- Ease

Look for opportunities to build both sides of your influencing style with each of your colleagues.

Are you prepared?

In order to influence anyone meaningfully and positively you need to have done your groundwork.

Unless you know where you stand and what your aims are, then there is no way you can move anyone else in the direction you desire.

- Can you place your colleague in your universe of influence? (Step 1)
- Have you defined your unique positive purpose? (Step 5)
- Do you know what skills and attributes make you credible? (Step 5)
- Have you used active verbs to define the personal impact you desire? (Step 6)

These ideas are fundamental to ensuring that, generally, you have a positive influence on those around you. These techniques both place you in a universe of influence and give you a meaningful orientation within it.

Once the general background is in place, the next step is to identify one specific, clear objective for the colleague in question.

What do you need from them?

Influencing is more specific than simply communicating successfully. To influence well, you need to have a goal in mind. There needs to be a specific purpose.

Are you communicating well?

As you'll have realised from reading this book, communicating well is a subtle and multifaceted process.

In order to influence a colleague you need to be aware of all communication habits, and make sure that nothing is inhibiting your chances of success.

Begin by listening!

Each colleague will be different. If you listen for long enough you'll learn what they want and what motivates them. Once you have picked up this information you can use it to nurture the relationship between you.

Water-cooler moments

Small talk matters, it's the glue that holds relationships together. Make the most of any incidental meeting, at the water cooler or in the lift for instance, to apply a bit more of this glue. Connect with your colleagues when and where you can.

Remember, you're playing the long game here. By building successful communication over time, you'll be set up to influence well when you really need to.

Flex your communication style for each colleague

Everybody responds to something different in you. Make sure that you meet them in the way they like to be met.

Equally, you will be responding to something in them. The greatest rapport occurs when you are responding to the same element in each other.

A great way to ensure that you are flexing your communication to meet your stakeholder in the appropriate manner is to *match their mood*.

Breathe out and put aside your own feelings and emotional energy for a moment and turn on your receptive self. Listen to, look at and feel the emotional state of the person you are communicating with.

Allow their state to affect you; allow yourself to take on a little of their emotional energy and mood. It can help here to subtly match their posture, tone of voice, eye contact and, crucially, breath quality. The breath often indicates the emotion.

This matching establishes a subtle physical and emotional 'bridge' between you and them. Once you're tuned in you can take the conversation in any direction you like.

What are they looking for in you?

- **Humour**
- **Clarity** – of thought or intention
- **Management** – helping them with action planning and targets
- **Friendship** – equal-status sharing of thoughts and feelings
- **Visionary imagination** – imagining what could be in the future
- **Logical persuasion** – facts and data

- **Collaboration** – searching for joint solutions
- **Status** – your ability to influence within the organisation
- **Coaching** – counselling, help with their needs and concerns
- **Energy or enthusiasm**

There are many potential answers to the above question, but the key is to be attuned to your colleagues.

Unless you are simply managing someone by diktat, then communicating effectively within the parameters of a meaningful relationship is the best way to influence a colleague.

Skill 3

Influencing in a meeting

'I am ready to disclaim my opinion, even of yesterday, even of 10 minutes ago, because all opinions are relative. One lives in a field of influences, one is influenced by everyone one meets, everything is an exchange of influences, all opinions are derivative. Once you deal a new deck of cards, you've got a new deck of cards.'

Peter Brook, theatre and film director

Are you prepared?

What preparation can you do for the meeting? Have you kept up to date with any papers/correspondence leading up to the meeting? Are you clear on your goals and do you already have an idea of the goals of others?

That first question again – 'What preparation *can* you do for the meeting? You can only be prepared to a degree. Preparedness must be balanced with 'aliveness' – being open and ready to communicate in the moment. Much as a theatre director should avoid marking up a script with blocking and interpretive marks before rehearsal begins, so should you enter a meeting in an open state of mind.

One area that you can prepare is practising your awareness of your own non-verbal influence (as in Step 2).

Work towards feeling comfortable with the following; perhaps focus on one change in your style at each meeting:

- Increase your awareness of your patterns – be they speech or movement, gesture or posture (e.g. do you sit back on your chair in a way that could be perceived as disengaged or do you have a distracting habit of fiddling with a notebook/pen or, even worse, some kind of phone/tablet/laptop?).

- Do you give full focus and attention to the speaker? Don't worry about trying to 'show them that you are listening' – instead simply listen. As you do this, your natural signals will be picked up by the speaker – they will know you are engaged.

- When you are speaking, have you thought about how you can 'cast your net'? If the meeting is with more than one person, aim to spread your communication out equally. Even if the particular comments are aimed at one individual, involve others through gentle, relaxed but mobile eye contact.

- Consider your level of confidence. Act confidently. Even if you are not feeling on top of the world today, fool your brain into an improved confident state by sitting upright, looking strong, present, receptive and attentive. Look alive.

All of these are areas of preparation. They are things that you can practise and see yourself achieving way in advance of the meeting itself. (For more on confidence refer back to Step 4.)

Is there a relationship?

What do you know? Who do you know?

How would you describe the relationship? Where does it sit on the swingometer between personal and professional?

Is it a first encounter? What can you do to maximise your first impression?

Make sure you work through the short exercise in Step 7, examining the differences between the *personal* and *work* versions of you. Perhaps aim for a little more parity, allowing the relationships to be strengthened by letting more of the *personal* version of you out.

The power to influence is usually best played as 'the long game', so see every meeting as an opportunity to really get to know the attendees. Build relationships, build trust.

Are you communicating well?

What do you want them to think, feel, do?

How many times have you been to what you regard as a pointless meeting? So, have a point even if those others attending do not!

Use think, feel, do from Step 6 to clarify the point of the meeting for you. Even if it is as simple as:

> *think* about your position in the team;
>
> *feel* motivated to improve it;
>
> *do* take notice of the relationship dynamics in the group.

At least this approach avoids meetings for meetings' sake.

Cut to the chase

Be prepared to do exactly that. As if you are telling a story, be ready to lose the preamble and cut to the chase scene. Be concise – if you only had one minute, what would the purpose of the meeting boil down to – what is the core?

Highly illogical

Consider also balancing your communication approach for the Kirks and Spocks in the room. Engage them in the way you are learning they like to be engaged. In a first encounter, balance 50:50. It will probably be a little more formal, but be careful not to neuter your personality. Aim to know them and for them to know you.

The weight of the world

In this fast-paced, time-poor world, meetings can be an irritant and stressful. In times of stress it is especially important to keep a check on how this can affect your communication. Learn to take a little more control of how you and your state of mind are perceived.

It is common to see people rubbing their shoulders when tense; a result of holding your shoulders up to protect your neck. Drop them. Sit or stand upright but drop your shoulders.

Breaking that tension cycle will have a pleasing effect upon others as they see you as more relaxed, confident and open.

Next time you have a meeting scheduled (perhaps one you are not looking forward to!), put time aside to work on the 'presence' exercises in Step 4.

Influencing senior management

Are you prepared?

You only get the occasional glimpse of senior management, and senior management only get the occasional glimpse of you. These glimpses are where you have the most to gain . . . and lose.

In an instant, people will form an impression of you, and that impression may be lasting, so you'd better make it a good one!

The only way to ensure the impression you have in those glimpses is good is to be prepared.

You need to be perceived as someone with values, integrity and purpose by those senior to you. They are looking for meaningful contributors to the team; members whom they can rely on to energise and motivate others.

Before going any further, make sure that you have all these fundamentals under your belt:

- Have you defined your unique positive purpose? (Step 5)
- Do you know what skills and attributes make you credible? (Step 5)
- Have you written the biography of your skills and strengths? (Step 9)
- Have you worked on your personal pitch? (Step 9)

By bringing your professional self into focus like this, you enable others to see you clearly too. With senior managers only seeing you in short glimpses, it's essential that they are able instantly to perceive what you stand for and what qualities you possess.

Is there a relationship?

Your relationship with senior managers can be distant, especially if they don't share the same office space with you every day. If this is the case, then you may need to be more strategic about your influencing.

There will often be people in your office who are senior to you, and it is those people who may be able to provide access to those senior to them.

Have a look at your universe of influence (Step 1) and pick out the most senior colleagues who fall within your inner orbit. Of these, with whom do you have the closest relationships?

You need to identify those who can help you influence deeper into your universe. Build your alliances wisely.

And play the long game (Step 10). It can take years to influence significantly those senior to you. You need to demonstrate your skill, integrity and efficacy over time. Take every opportunity you can to show them how well you can do. Get into the habit of saying 'yes' as opposed to shying away and hoping somebody picks up on your concealed brilliance.

Have the courage to show off a little! But be judicious enough to know that less is sometimes more. It's another fine balance you're trying to strike.

Are you communicating well?

More than anyone else, senior managers tend to be time poor. There's no room for waffle. You need to have done most of your thinking before you get in the room with them.

Know your stuff

They're looking for expertise and knowledge. It's always an opportunity to demonstrate your value to the team. While this kind of deep preparation takes place over years, there's still no harm in quickly organising your thoughts and focusing on your core abilities and strengths in the short lift-ride to the office. Make the most of your time.

Be honest

Honesty is essential. People can always tell if you're blagging! Sometimes it is stronger to say 'I don't know, but I'll find out' than to make something up to save face. As long as you have values and purpose, the occasional hole in your knowledge isn't such a big deal.

Trust your expertise and experience to see you through.

Be timely

Pick your moments well. There's no point in trying to influence someone who hasn't got the time to listen. Meetings with senior managers may only be called with a specific purpose and agenda in mind and they won't appreciate you going off piste if time is tight.

Be concise

Get to the point by the quickest route possible. And don't be afraid of silence; if there's nothing to say, don't say anything – waffle is your worst enemy.

Present options and thoughts, don't ask for solutions

Don't burden senior managers with more problems to solve; they've got enough on their plates already. Present considered options and possible solutions to the issues at hand. Make yourself useful!

Be flexible and ready to collaborate if the chance arises

Again, this calls for you to deploy fine judgement. If the opportunity to collaborate and generate new ideas with senior management presents itself, be prepared to grasp it with both hands. These moments can be few and far between; they're like rare jewels.

Never switch off from the possibility that a chance might arise.

Embody relaxed aliveness

What you say about yourself non-verbally matters (Step 2). Too little tension and you'll come across as though you don't care; too much tension and you'll appear too anxious and lacking in confidence.

1. Be relaxed, but alive. Be present.

2. Centre your breath.

3. Release your neck and shoulders.

4. Sit alert at the front edge of your chair.

5. Be still and focused.

Skill 5

Influencing a client

Are you prepared?

Whether buying pet supplies on eBay, choosing a hotel using TripAdvisor or a carpenter on Rated People, it's all about trust. Would you buy a car online from a vendor with zero feedback? Would you risk thousands on the dream honeymoon without researching first?

Trust is more important than ever as it's we, the customers, who hold much more of the power now. We are wise to sales methods of yesteryear (door-to-door, telesales, spam adverts). Even a sniff of hoodwinking or coercion will have us slamming doors, hanging up or adding to junk folders without a second thought. As the consumer, client or customer we can access that knowledge at our fingertips and now there is no going back. Assessing trust and making purchasing decisions armed with this digital power is the norm for most nowadays. The power to find the best price on, say, flights and hotel or car insurance is no longer the privilege of the holiday salesperson or broker. So, think about how this affects you as supplier and about your relationship with clients, both potential and established.

What is their experience of you?

You should obsess over the customer journey – like we do. The whole journey. This is not to say that you become slave to the client and attend to their every need in a desperate fashion, but 'them clients' can be a fickle bunch and because information and choice are powers they happily wield they can drop you pretty easily!

How you shape the customer journey should be underpinned by knowing your core – your positive purpose (as outlined in Step 5). If you define your positive purpose, you'll find it easier to maintain continuity for the clients. They know what you stand for and what to expect from you. They become familiar with the language you use to talk about yourself and the product/service, and trust that 'what they see truly is what they get' . . . YOU!

Remember this is a book requiring *action*. It's not a theory, it's a guide to best practice, so go ahead now and perform the biography and timeline exercise in Step 5. If you can't do it now, stick it in your diary and underline it as a priority.

Use this exercise as a way of improving every aspect of the customer journey.

Is there a relationship?

As a leading provider of soft-skills training in the UK, we are fully aware that we have to utilise LinkedIn and the like, keep our site up to date and relevant, use social media and stay current, just to keep our heads above water in a saturated market-place. Most of our new clients come through word-of-mouth recommendation. The third party has often laid the groundwork for the relationship; that relationship is built on trust. As an HR manager, you may be reluctant or even terrified at the prospect of switching suppliers for training. There is a risk, a big risk, that you could look very foolish. We always nod to this in our initial conversations, we highlight our understanding of this risk and make it clear that we will do all we can to negate the risk. Indeed, if we are not the provider for you, we will say so.

There it is really: transparency and empathy. Try not to think of a business relationship as too different from that of a friendship or partnership with a loved one.

Balanced approach

Can you improve your understanding of how people want to be communicated with . . . short succinct email/phone calls or face to face for detail? We're back with Kirk and Spock.

It's all about balance here:

- **Balance of pathos and logos (heart and mind)** – build the relationship by understanding the ways they prefer to communicate.
- **Balance of extrovert and introvert*** – avoiding becoming overly assertive.
- **Balance of listening and responding** – of questioning and stating.

People buy from people. Do they? We tend to buy anonymously online or wrestle with the self-service checkouts in the supermarket. However, we assume here that you have or can have a human-to-human relationship. The human connection can make or break the relationship with the organisation. Understanding your positive purpose and, again, balancing this with the understanding of your client will serve to build the trust and strengthen all of the relationships (you + client,

*Discover more about being ambervert (the selling state sitting between extrovert and introvert) from Daniel H. Pink's *Made to Sell*.

client + organisation, client + product/service, you + product/ service). You become your product/service.

Are you communicating well?

Danger, danger! From this day forth vow to be fully aware of your own 'assumptive behaviour'. In Step 7 we talk of the assumptions we can make when communicating and these assumptions (a guessing game that can have serious ramifications) can steer you onto the wrong path and ruin the client relationship.

**Assumptions
Ahead!**

Stack what you *know* about your client up against what you *think you know*. Stop finishing their sentences for them and focus on the listening and making sure they *know* you are listening.

Assumptions can include:

- understanding;
- thoughts;
- feelings;
- knowledge;
- context;
- interest;
- humour;
- appropriateness;
- preferences;
- familiarity – friendliness;
- frame of mind.

You may find it helpful when focusing on a particular client relationship to list assumptions that you make when communicating with them.

Time is on your side

'But I finish their sentences because I know them by now, I know what they are going to say and surely this illustrates how well I know them . . . anyhow it speeds things up!'

Assumptions can often be a false economy. Those seconds you save in finishing sentences for your client (verbalising your assumptions) can lead to frustration if you have indeed made the incorrect assumption. Maybe giving them the opportunity to actually voice their concerns, following through on the process of thought to speech, is good for them. Allow them to speak their mind. Resist the need to rush through, allow space in the conversation, allow moments of stillness, of silence, of consideration.

When you do speak, make sure that you:

- **Question** to seek out more information on what they *want* or *need* from you.
- **State** with reassurance that everything you do is to meet those *wants* or *needs* as best you can.

Lastly, **don't be afraid of questioning**. We can often feel that if we ask the wrong question it will expose our lack of knowledge – the knowledge we are expected to have or that our role demands.

Build with care

So, now that you truly understand your client's needs – are you showing you understand?

To do this, keep the client up to date – be regular and concise. Use the pathos/logos balance – know by now whether they favour the facts/figure details or just top-line progress.

Client relations are delicate. It may take years to build the client relationship. You may be taking over as a representative who is now responsible for that relationship. It only takes one bad experience for the house of cards to fall. That bad experience may be due to *your* response – a response not designed to serve the needs of the client but to satisfy your need to respond in the moment. So take a breath and wait.

Avoid responding when you should be listening.

Influencing in an interview

Are you prepared?

'Fail to prepare, prepare to fail.' Never is this truer than with an interview.

There are two types of preparation for an interview: background and foreground. The background preparation you need to do has been widely covered elsewhere in this book (see Steps 5, 7 and 9).

Before going any further make sure you have:

- defined your skills and qualities;
- defined your unique positive purpose;
- written your skills biography.

Without these in place you have only shaky foundations upon which to build. You must know what you *stand* for before you begin to consider the specifics of the interview. This bigger picture informs the specific interaction of the interview; without this bigger picture your presentation lacks depth.

Once you have these key ideas consolidated, you can move onto foreground preparation – the specifics.

First, make sure you have your personal brand and pitch on the tip of your tongue (Step 9).

Reduce the language

By clarifying your three-sentence pitch and, if possible, reducing your personal brand to a single word, you are not only preparing to *sound* focused during the interview, you are also telling your mind to concentrate on the essentials. Just like a mantra, the more you repeat it the greater its influence on your thinking and the greater its influence during the interview.

Rehearse, rehearse, rehearse

There is no better preparation for an interview, or a performance of any kind, than live rehearsal.

And that's the key – the words you say and the movements of your body go together. Your language inhabits your body and infuses it with meaning and purpose.

Make sure you role-play answering potential interview questions out loud and preferably up on your feet. This rehearsed animation will flow through during the interview, even if the interview is static.

Use your imagination

The mind and the body are interwoven and just as the body can lead the mind, so the mind can lead the body. Mental rehearsal is a great preparation tool.

Play the film of the interview in your mind's eye. Imagine yourself in the interview room, sitting upright in the chair, looking relaxed and easily engaged with your interviewers.

Picture the interviewers asking a question and see yourself taking your time to answer in a calm and thoughtful manner.

Finally, imagine the interviewer asking you a very difficult question – what might that question be? And visualise yourself answering that question intelligently, remaining composed and grounded with your breath connected to your centre.

Revisit and replay this mental film as often as you can in the days leading up to your interview.

Is there a relationship?

An interview is the beginning of a potentially exciting and life-changing relationship.

Imagine the future relationship

As part of your preparation and research you may have begun to imagine working for the company, you have begun to form a possible new relationship in your mind. This imagined relationship is the relationship you want the interviewers to engage with and join you in. We return again to the imagination's power to inform and shape the future.

Use a timeline extending 10 years into the future to plot your prospective relationship with the company. Fill in as many details as you can – possible achievements, potential relationships, deployment of skills.

Imagining a successful future with the company is the first step to making it happen.

Get off on the right foot

It's important to make the right impression to set this new relationship off in the right direction. Pulling no punches, it's important that the interviewers like you and feel that you would get on well with colleagues. That doesn't mean you have to be an extrovert, or a social dynamo. It's more subtle than that.

You need to demonstrate sensitivity and flexibility. The ability to adapt and respond to a diverse range of people is what matters.

Show curiosity. At the start of any relationship it is as important for you to find out as much about them as for them to find out about you. Use the interview to gain as much understanding of the company and the role as you can. Your aim is to understand as much as you possibly can.

By shifting your focus slightly from 'Am I right for this job?' to 'Is this job right for me?', you also ease the pressure of the interview a little.

Are you communicating well?

Be positive

Positivity comes in many forms. You can be interested, curious and keen to learn. You can be informed, expert and driven. You can be bright, responsive and full of ideas. You can be physically present and 'alive'. Ideally, you can be all these things at once.

However positivity manifests in you, use it.

The way you make people feel matters. If you are sluggish, dour and uninspired then you will make others feel this way too.

Find your spark and use it to ignite the interview.

Listen

Always balance your outward communication with deep listening. By listening with a genuine desire to understand, you demonstrate depth and you open your mind to new possibilities.

Only through listening during an interview does the interview stand any chance of taking flight in an unexpected and positive manner, rather than remaining nothing more than a series of questions and answers.

Be open. Pick up on what you hear. What do the interviewers seem interested in? What makes them tick? Can you find any immediate common ground?

Make sure you are listening, and not pretending to listen in order to show your listening skills! The only listening skill of any worth is the ability to really listen with desire to understand.

Be concise

Don't waffle. Allow silence. Make your words count.

Be future focused

Use the imagined reality of yourself in the role to frame your conversation. Wherever possible, act and speak as if you are already in the role and performing well.

Start your sentences with

'I will . . . '

For example:

'I will encourage my team of designers to pay greater attention to the client brief.'

As opposed to:

'I would encourage my team of designers to pay greater attention to the client brief.'

It's subtle, but it begins to establish a new reality.

Help them understand you

Remember, the interviewees are trying to form an opinion about your suitability for the role, so help them out by giving as much information about yourself as possible.

Use every answer you give to their questions to illustrate something of your working style, your personality or your skills.

Consider your main attributes before you go into the interview room, and use them to frame every answer you give. This will leave the interviewers with a coherent lasting impression of you.

For example:

Interviewer: 'Tell me about your project management experience?'

Response 1: 'Well, I've managed projects for the past two years both in the publishing industry and in design. The last one I managed was a six-month project for a major high street brand.'

That's pretty dull and doesn't really give the interviewer any information about you, only information about the projects you were involved in.

Response 2: 'For me, the most important element in managing any project is communication. I always communicate regularly with all the stakeholders in the project and ensure I understand their needs up front. Only then will I be able to bring them altogether to get the project done. A recent example of this is . . . '

This second response is framed with an illustration of who you are and what you do, giving the interviewers an insight into how you would approach the role on offer.

Influencing in a phone call

Are you prepared?

The question really is – is telephone the right medium for this conversation? If it's unavoidable, prepare using the techniques in this book in the same way you would for other encounters.

As you would for face-to-face meetings, prepare with an appropriate environment. Use a space that will enable you to focus without interruption and think without distraction.

Choose the posture that you think will work for the type of call. In Step 3 we talk about how the smile behind the voice can have a real effect; the same goes for posture. You wouldn't wheel a bed in to an office and conduct a meeting from the foetal position, all snuggled up, would you?! If you are working from home, shower, have breakfast and dress for the day. Business is business. This simple tenet will do wonders for the work–life balance of homeworkers too.

Plan intention using *think, feel, do* in the same way you would for a face-to-face meeting, but also remember that this is a conversation, not a lecture or a presentation. Be flexible and allow for two-way flow.

Aim for them to *think* about your contribution to the call, to *feel* listened to and to *do* want to speak to you again because of this experience.

If you have very specific objectives, perhaps even practise the words out loud and allow your whole body to follow. Stand engaged when rehearsing and allow for full congruency – use your hands to gesture, your face to express and your voice to show connection to the objectives. It's all very well saying you are 'very excited about this new opportunity', but does it show in your monotonous delivery?

Is there a relationship?

It is clearly very, very different when you have an existing relationship – you understand each other's speech patterns, tonality, sense of humour and you can picture the individual in person. See each call as an opportunity to cultivate relationships.

A simple approach to building the relationship is to remember this:

instead of being interesting – be interested.

Are you communicating well?

So are you physically present – in the same way as you would be in a face-to-face meeting? Having clarified your intentions, be ready now to listen to theirs.

Silence is golden

Silence can be ambiguous in a call with the loss of non-verbal acknowledgements, so be in the habit of summarising and voicing understanding. However, don't get carried away! Appreciate the silence – the space for thought and reflection. Choose to be comfortable with silence, with space.

Cull and void

Cull your unproductive filler language – resist the urge to fill the void. Instead *allow* the void – the empty space.

Listen not only to the other party but to yourself. Start this today – in the next phone call you have, improve your awareness of just how many times you are talking just for the sake of filling the void.

'Don't fear the tumbleweed moment!'

Shift your focus from talking to listening. Increase the efficiency of the call by really listening with a desire to understand.

Next time you have a call coming up (any call, not just the important ones, as this gives you a chance to practise your telephone technique) read over this list and see if you can tick each box:

Before you dial are you clear about what you want from the call?	✓
Are you focusing on just the phone call without distraction (e.g. gadgets)?	✓
Are you avoiding mumbling – using your voice confidently with energy to the end of the line?	✓
Are you 'alive and present' in the call like you would be face to face?	✓
Should you perhaps stand and be grounded?	✓
Are you leaving space for the communication to work? (Be comfortable with pauses either from you or them.)	✓

Take note

If you have not already, try this. During the call, organise your thoughts and note theirs. One of the reasons we trample over each other in a phone call is a fear of forgetting to say something we deem important that very second. It can usually wait.

Divide a page and on one side *make notes* of things you want to say – those important reactions that come to you when the call is in progress and when the other party is speaking. On the other side *take notes* of what is clearly important to them. This will help you to remember to address these and make them feel truly listened to. Make this a habit. Of course the advantage of having these notes after the call, summarising them, scanning them and referring to them will help make the next chapter of your communication seamless. You'll pick up where you left off – just like you do with a friend you rarely see. The relationship is being built.

Finally, improvise! As communicators we improvise all day long and generally we're pretty good at it. We certainly don't walk around with a script of the conversation we are about to have, so be ready to listen, to accept and build conversation. Even if you disagree over a point you can still aim to give the whole call a *yes . . . and* feel (Step 8).

Influencing in a crisis

Are you prepared?

Whether you are managing a team, or simply a member of a team, when an unexpected emergency strikes the quality of your preparation will be put to the test.

Of course, the nature of an unexpected event means you can't necessarily be prepared for its occurrence.

The key to surviving a crisis is to have your groundwork in place, both by building relationships within your team and by learning how best to manage your own stress.

Use phases of calm – when it's business as usual – to nurture relationships with colleagues. If you are in management your team need to trust you, they need to feel safe in the knowledge that if the going gets tough they could rely on your support and navigation.

Furthermore, *you* need to feel safe in the knowledge that if the going gets tough you could both support yourself emotionally and rely upon yourself to provide direction.

This is where all your work on your personal biography, skills biography and connection to your authentic self comes into play (Step 9).

You need to:

- **Be authentic:** listen to yourself and pay attention to your own feelings; communicate with your team from these genuine feelings. You are your primary resource.

- **Reflect upon and trust your own experience:** your personal story and skills biography is an essential tool. You can only draw upon your own experience, so make sure you bring it to the fore.
- **Consider your team:** they are your secondary resource. In times of business as usual, reflect upon your team; in a crisis, each one of them will be looking for something different from you to help them through. Who can you rely on? Who has personal resilience? Who will need help handling the pressure? Who will need focusing? Who should you leave to their own devices?

Manage your own stress

Know yourself. Know where you find support, and make sure that in a crisis you lean on those bases.

To have a positive influence, you need to stay centred and balanced. If you are reeling out of control, your influence will only be unsettling to others.

Make sure you do the basics: eat well, sleep well, breathe well . . . and switch off the email after work.

If it's ruining your health, it's just not worth it.

Is there a relationship?

Without some level of trust in your workplace relationships, it will be very hard to wield significant influence in a time of crisis. This trust takes time to build, which is an important reminder: influencing is not a series of quick fixes, it is a long-term activity requiring personal commitment and investment. This long-term investment builds a big reservoir of trust.

In the most difficult moments, as a manager, it is important to be present, to engage with your staff. Do not disappear into your bunker, do not close down. Stay open.

Show concern. Check in with people. Communicate. Ask them what help they need to help them through. It may be as simple as providing free breakfast at work during the week.

All these little things add up. During times of greatest stress, you need to listen with closer attention than usual to the unique needs of each colleague. You need to tune into the emotional state of your staff, and act as a lightning rod to diffuse any excess charge.

Here are a few good ways to diffuse an emotional charge:

- humour – allow laughter;
- getting to the root of the issue, talking it out;
- providing perspective – it's never the end of the world;
- giving clear direction;
- listening;
- reminding your team of the common goal;
- taking responsibility for the issue at hand, thereby easing the pressure on your team.

The good news is, not only does a crisis test your workplace relationships to the maximum, it also provides an opportunity to form new and lasting relationships quickly. Relationships forged in the full heat of the furnace can be the strongest, so make sure you capitalise on these opportunities when they arise.

Are you communicating well?

Communicate, communicate, communicate.

If you're not communicating in a crisis, you're not being influential. In fact, you run the risk of things going seriously off the rails.

Your team will be looking for clear direction, so provide it. Providing a daily focus for the team is sometimes more important than the focus itself for holding things together. If the direction proves to be the wrong one, you can always change it.

Establishing a secure holding state enables staff to continue to function while a permanent solution is found.

Be clear and decisive

Offer clear direction and decisive action as soon as it is possible to do so and be generous with the information that you have. Nothing breeds distrust faster than people feeling in the dark or, even worse, disregarded.

Don't put up a front

People can tell if you're faking it.

If you're swirling in inner panic, it's better to take a few moments to regain your composure, to connect with your centred breath (Step 4), than to put on a brave face. Otherwise the cracks will appear and this deep anxiety will infect the rest of your team.

Conversely, as long as your centre is calm, and you fundamentally trust yourself, there's no harm in showing a little agitation or anxiety. If anything, this will reassure your staff as they see that their feelings of stress are normal under the circumstances and that it's possible to function effectively, perhaps even more effectively than usual, despite them.

Finally, smile when you can – it shows everyone you're coping!

Skill 9

Influencing in a presentation

'The most important thing for me is that it wasn't boring'

Are you prepared?

Hunching over your laptop, creating a sparkly PowerPoint is *not* working on your presentation. It's a tool that you may choose to use to assist you in delivering your message.

Get up on your feet and speak out loud. Learn to appear comfortable with being uncomfortable. Presenting demands a degree of performance energy. This is not to say that you should adopt a different personality, wear a costume and act, but we don't want to be bored! It's you but it's the performer in you. The performance is genuine, it's natural, it's you through and through. So, get up on your feet and speak the words out loud.

> *'Readiness is all.'*

Sage advice from Shakespeare's *Hamlet*

Presentations are fantastic opportunities to flex your influencing skills.

You must decide upon *intention* for every part of the presentation and if you have planned and rehearsed well enough it should be seen as an invigorating and exciting communication.

On our presentation skills training programme 'Art of Presenting', which has been delivered to thousands of staff at all levels in all sectors, we give great focus to intention. The feedback since

2006 has nearly always been that the presenter learns to focus on intention rather than worrying about their nerves and how those nerves show themselves in front of an audience. Instead of something to fear, presenting then becomes an experience to enjoy.

Presenting/public speaking can indeed be very stressful. We worry about a great deal of things (many of which are beyond our control) but if we define our intentions then not only is this the key to dynamic, focused and interesting presentations but also the key to creating the presentation content.

At the planning stages of your presentation, begin with intention and work through the 'active verb' approach as detailed in Step 6. As you decide upon the changes in intention, the presentation almost writes itself. If you are reviewing an existing presentation and cannot decide upon the underlying verb (the effect you want to have on the audience) then perhaps it needs cutting.

At every stage of your presentation you must decide what you want your audience to think, to feel, to do.

Consider this

A troupe of actors decide upon a play to perform in six weeks' time. The play is cast and the date is set. 'See you in six weeks then at 7:00 pm!'

Oh dear. The play has been written and the venue organised. The tickets have been sold and the audience are eagerly anticipating the performance.

But what about the rehearsal? Ridiculous isn't it. It is never enough to read through your notes on the train heading to the presentation.

So get up on your feet and rehearse!

Now that you have created the content by deciding upon intentions, try out the language. As you stand and move and speak, all should work together congruently. Intention informs delivery – all else will follow. Allow yourself to have an experience of performing.

And remember, we don't want to watch you rehearsing. Build your sense of confidence by getting the mistakes out in the rehearsal phase. This is what all professional performers do, no matter what the discipline.

Script	Supporting image or text displayed	Verb information delivery
A handwriting font is perfect for getting that freestyle look or for making an art journal page look like you actually wrote it for real with an actual pen.		WELCOME
A handwriting font is perfect for getting that freestyle look or for making an art journal page look like you actually wrote it for real with an actual pen.		INFORM
A handwriting font is perfect for getting that freestyle look or for making an art journal page look like you actually wrote it for real with an actual pen.		INSPIRE
A handwriting font is perfect for getting that freestyle look or for making an art journal page look like you actually wrote it for real with an actual pen.		EXCITE

Is there a relationship?

Presenting is two-way. It is not a lecture, it is a conversation.

> 'At a recent presentation to 40+ people I gave up on the slide show, finding that they restricted my train of thought and didn't deliver what I sensed the audience were expecting. I went off-piste, much to my colleagues worry, and talked directly from my experience and related that to theirs. The mood in the room changed dramatically and the engagement became much more rewarding. The Q&A more constructive.'

Slides and handouts can kill the presenter–audience relationship. As you become more experienced and confortable with presenting you should aim to cultivate the relationship by 'relating'. Establish a connection with the audience.

Are you communicating well?

Use the multitude of techniques from Part 1 and see presenting as an opportunity to try them out. Pause now and refer to Step 3. To improve and perfect your influencing when presenting take any opportunity you can to get up in front of an audience. Really try out each of the techniques and skills talked about in the earlier part of this book and see what works for you.

> *'Suit the action to the word, the word to the action, with this special observance, that you o'erstep not the modesty of nature.'*

> Shakespeare's *Hamlet* giving advice to the court performers

What do I do with my hands?

Are you 'comforting' yourself – maybe we as an audience are not interested in watching you comfort yourself. Many inexperienced presenters fall into the trap of using repeated gestures and non-verbal habits to simply make themselves feel more secure in this nerve-racking scenario.

Make certain that:

- you are not performing patterns – physical or vocal;
- you are not 'hands in pockets' purely because you find it comforting;
- you are not exhibiting signs of wanting to escape – shrinking away or speeding up.

Influencing from the front (as leader)

Are you prepared?

Your entire life up until the point when you are called upon to lead is your preparation to be a leader.

No matter how early on in your career you are thrust into leadership, your experience is invaluable to you. Your experience, to that point, is yours and yours alone – and the lessons you have taken from it are yours too. Trust your experience. Trust your thoughts and feelings. Trust yourself – you have been asked to lead for a reason: you are ready for it.

Broad awareness

To be a successful, influential leader you first need to develop a broad awareness. It is part of your responsibility to hold the bigger picture, and its many permutations, in your mind. The more you reflect, the fewer blind spots you will have.

Refresh your universe of influence (Step 1).

Consider these areas:

- the company or organisation – its purpose and aims;
- the organisation's performance in the past five years;
- the company staff structure;
- the core company processes;
- key relationships, both those with you and those between others;

- the individual members of staff;
- yourself – your thoughts, your feelings, your ambitions, your strengths and weaknesses. Crucially, consider your work relationships – where can they be improved?

Be focused

By defining your positive purpose, your personal brand and your one-word slogan (Step 9), you not only build clarity of purpose into your thoughts and actions, you enable others to perceive you clearly as well.

By bringing your meaning into focus, you bring yourself into focus for others.

You will avoid blurred edges and present a sharply defined image to your staff and colleagues. This clear purpose will imbue your actions and interactions with an unshakable meaningfulness, and a leader's actions always have meaning. As a leader, every step you take in front of your colleagues is read for meaning. Make sure it's the meaning you want.

Common goal

Once you have set out your own purpose, the next step is to use it to motivate your team around a common goal.

The strength of your personal convictions has the power to get your team all pulling together, and in the same direction. However, the real power lies in uniting your staff around a set of shared goals or principles. For your staff to take responsibility and be proactive in the fulfilment of these goals they need to play a part in creating them.

Avoid imposing your thinking too firmly; instead allow the team to find its common purpose under your watchful guidance.

It is your job to ensure that gradually, over time, the team coalesces around a meaningful, shared purpose.

Is there a relationship?

As a leader, and an influencer, *people* are what matter. It is, after all, people you are leading. Not projects, not data, not work flows, not plans. People. Without people to lead, you are not a leader.

Place people, and relationships, at the centre of your leadership. If a relationship breaks down, you lose your power to influence and lead. This is the greatest challenge of leadership; you need to develop the flexibility and empathetic skills to identify with and communicate with a wide range of people, some of whom will be very different from you.

As a leader it is your responsibility to put your personal preferences to one side and adapt in order to make difficult relationships work. This doesn't mean compromising your principles, or letting others' set the agenda; it means having the self-awareness to know when you may be allowing your personal response to someone to interfere with your professional duty. And your professional duty requires that you find a way to connect.

People will follow you because they want to.

Personality

The most effective leaders allow their personality to shine through.

Richard Branson is a great example of an influential leader who allows himself to have fun in front of his staff and colleagues. He lets the more animated side of himself burst through on regular occasions, sharing his humour and charisma with his team. This, in turn, frees them to do the same, to invest themselves more fully in their work and work life.

Be genuine, authentic and interested in the people in your team; look to connect on a personal level where you can. The best leaders are fascinated by people, by what drives them, motivates them and brings the best performance from them.

Everybody you lead is an opportunity to learn.

Collaborate

The ability to collaborate and to get others to collaborate is a great leadership skill. As a leader you set the tone for your team, and by demonstrating the will and desire to collaborate you engender collaboration in others.

Your attitude, habits and behaviour form those of your team. Your team is made in your image.

Are you communicating well?

Embody confident ease

The most effective modern leaders not only embody confidence and purpose, they also embody ease. They take *their* time, and will not be rushed or pressured by anyone. They have the confidence to stick to their own agenda.

Indeed, the leader of the free world, Barack Obama – surely a man working under more pressure than anyone else on the planet – is a master of confident ease. His body is relaxed and centred at all times; and when the stakes are high, and his work is urgent, this urgency flows naturally through him rather than tangling him up in nerves and tension.

Ensure that you are communicating from a fully expanded physicality, with a centred breath and open voice (see Steps 2, 3 and 4).

Great leaders listen well

Listening is the key to understanding others; and the more you understand the people you lead, the more influential you become.

Make sure you create one-to-one opportunities to listen to your staff face to face, but also gently eavesdrop! Have your ears, eyes and awareness open wide and stay tuned in to the emotional tone of your workforce.

Monitor your impact

As leader you have the greatest impact and, therefore, you need to have the greatest awareness of your impact.

Every conversation you have will impact upon the person you have it with. What may seem a passing remark to you, could have a resounding impact on them.

You are significant.

Monitor your impact carefully and constantly recalibrate it to ensure you're making the right impression. Use your active verbs! (Step 6.)

Lead by example

Finally, lead by example.

Like a parent with a child, you model the behaviour you wish to see in others.

If you fly off the handle with rage, or drown in nerves, or look miserable at work, then you sap the energy and enthusiasm of others. If you aren't up for the day ahead, why should they be?

By employing all the leadership skills in this step, you *will* be setting a good example to your staff, but it's essential to remember the personal influence you wield simply by holding the position you hold.

Make it count.

Part 3

10 influencing challenges in action

How do I influence without 'treading on people's toes'?

If we are to think for a moment about actually 'treading on people's toes' then in order to do this we must be moving. Simply put, before moving forward with your idea you must stand still.

You must imagine what it is like to tread in other people's shoes to avoid treading on them. The key here is understanding their position, and this includes a full understanding of their barriers and the reasons for their possible opposition.

The mistake is to be overly assertive and ignore the position of others. It is not enough just to listen to their standpoint and then trample over it. They need to know that you really get their point of view.

Tips to treading carefully

Listen up

'I hear you, I hear you!'

'Yes, but are you listening?'

They are different. We hear all the time and we tune out. Listening goes one step further. Instead of working your way through your own thoughts, pay attention to the other party. You don't need to do anything to show them you are listening – just listen. Once you are sure they have had the full opportunity to voice their position you can gently reflect this back by summarising and showing understanding.

Acknowledge

When communicating with someone who is clearly in an opposing position, it can be difficult to acknowledge their position, especially if you passionately disagree. This is perhaps because we fear the other party will see our nodding and positive affirmative language as 'agreeing with them'. Free yourself from this worry by making the clear distinction between 'acknowledging' and 'agreeing'. Focus on letting them know that you have heard and understood their position. Their toes will be safe from harm and they will be more likely to afford you the same opportunity.

Challenge 2

How do I influence a diverse team?

All teams are diverse. There's no escaping the fact that everybody is different, no matter how subtle those differences appear to be; and you wouldn't want it any other way.

Very often, the strength of a team lies in its diversity.

Of course some teams instantly appear more diverse than others, especially if you're on the lookout for the diversity big hitters:

- ethnic
- cultural
- religious
- gender
- sexuality.

While these strands of diversity need to be noted and tended to, it's a mistake to assume that as long as you're ticking those boxes you're doing all you can. In fact, as individuals, we aren't necessarily defined by any of those common diversity badges.

And, as an influencer, what could be more ridiculous than planning a specific approach for 'all British Caucasian males' or 'all Afro-Caribbean Christian females'?

Fundamentally, the greatest indicators of diversity and difference lie at the level of the individual. As soon as you're applying any group identities, you're limiting your awareness of genuine, subtle difference.

Tips to influence a diverse team

Treat everyone as an individual

If this sounds obvious, that's because it is. But it's so easy to forget. The only way to truly influence anyone is to understand them first.

Everybody is different. The more you can learn about what makes a person tick, what inspires them and what they need, the greater your potential for having an impact.

It's also important to understand their relationship to the team dynamic. For some, being part of a team is stressful, while others thrive on being a member of a vibrant, energetic group. Remember that no team is complete without this range of personalities; none is necessarily any better than another.

The key is to develop the team to ensure that it caters for everyone.

Keep the team in check

A team will develop a personality of its own, often led by those with the strongest personalities within the group. For example, you may have a very noisy, talkative team or, conversely, a silent team, reluctant to share information.

Watch out for these currents and work to challenge them. The prevailing culture of a team can dominate, causing individuals to behave in a way that doesn't suit them and doesn't help anyone. Individuals become trampled under the feet of the stampeding team.

Keep your 'group think' antennae switched on, and when you feel that a course of action is being pursued purely because the historic team dynamic dictates, that's the time to offer an alternative.

Unify under a common goal

As well as being made up of various unique individuals, each with their own experience, opinions and needs, a team, by definition, also inhabits a common ground and is formed around a shared goal.

If the diversity within the team is threatening to tear the team to pieces, you need to redirect people's focus and energy to the common goal.

The common goal is the unifying force. Define it and keep it in mind at all times.

How do I turn around a failing presentation?

Clearly, seeing as public speaking is up there with death as a major human fear, it is understandable that a presentation that is failing can be an excruciating nightmare for both presenter and audience. You've thoroughly planned your presentation but now, with all eyes on you, something is not going to plan.

Where does this fear originate from and why does it fill us with such a strong sense of dread? Being exposed as failing in front of an audience in this way we fear the threat to our status and, on a primal level, being ostracised from our social group. This, of course, will not happen. Know this.

We put ourselves under immense pressure to be funny, entertaining, dynamic, professional, all-knowing. . . no wonder. So stop there and give yourself a break.

We as an audience expect the 'professional' bit, but not for you to wow us with all the other qualities. These will come with time.

Professionals get it wrong too. If you can bear it, look up film director Michael Bay's anxiety-driven flee from the stage during a press conference. You can't help but feel sorry for him, it could happen to anyone. As we watch this we almost feel what he is feeling. We can take from this the certainty that your audience wants you to succeed, rather than feel your failure.

In both sections on presenting in this book (Step 4 and Skill 9), we continually emphasise the need to prepare and rehearse. The preparation and rehearsal, though, is not specific to a single presentation, it comes from developing your skill as a communicator over months and years; taking any opportunity you can to stand up and be heard. So instead of shying away, seek out and embrace any chance to flex this muscle because when it does go wrong (and it will), experience will get you through.

When you are rehearsing, think of it as developing flexibility and not rigidity. We never want to hear you read your presentation (learnt or not) word for word. If the presentation is a framework, and the structure in which pretty much anything can happen is flexible, then really it can't go wrong.

Tips to keeping a presentation alive

Come back to earth

Work through the earlier exercises on breath and physical grounding to become your own personal expert and saviour in times of stress. Pause, remember where you are and why. Slow it down and return to a sense of physical neutrality: two feet firmly planted on the ground, hip-width apart. Refocus on your breath, low and deep, and drop your shoulders.

If you use notes, write in little reminders on breath and physicality.

Be empathetic, not neurotic

How do you know the presentation is failing? Is it because you are focusing on the glassy stare from a single member of the audience? Are you reading into this signal and others as evidence of boredom or confusion, and therefore convincing yourself in that moment that the presentation is failing?

Recast your net over the audience; widen your focus to include those at the periphery too. You prepared well and you understand your positive purpose, and the presentation is fuelled by the active verbs that inspired the writing in the first place. Return to these and, with an awareness of the audience, inject life into each new section. Turn this feeling around and see it as a change of gear. Focus on your message.

Return to the core

If you've prepared thoroughly, you'll know what the key message of your presentation is. You'll be able to sum it up in one sentence.

Now is the time to use it! If you're lost or have been thrown off course, reorientate and take control of your message again.

How do I influence when there is conflict in my team?

At its simplest level, conflict is a breakdown of communication between two people. Your job is to reconnect those people, to bridge the gap that has emerged between them and that they are struggling to bridge for themselves.

If we imagine communication as a flow of both ideas and feelings between people, a breakdown in communication often occurs when the flow of feelings clogs up the flow of ideas.

Anger, irritation, jealousy, anxiety, fear, resentment – the list goes on – once negative feeling has accumulated it forms a barrier that must be broken down before meaningful communication can recommence.

Tips for resolving conflict

Listen and clarify understanding

Conflict is where your listening skills come to the fore. Listen to each participant in the conflict, with your sole desire being to understand their point of view.

Do not seek to change their mind, offer an alternative opinion or assert your view. Unless people feel heard and understood, they will not be prepared to change their behaviour.

Once you've listened, you must then check your understanding by summarising what you believe they have said and asking if that is correct. For example:

> 'As I understand it you are annoyed because the extra work you did on the last project was not appreciated so now you don't feel like meeting the high expectations of your manager? Is that correct?'

Then allow yourself to be guided to a more nuanced understanding until you are both satisfied that the situation is comprehended.

Diffuse emotion and create neutral space

Simply by listening and understanding you will diffuse some of the tension and negative feeling, which will begin to create a neutral space for fresh connection to occur in.

All new communication requires open space to flourish. Communication occurs in the space between people.

In a conflict, there is often no intellectual or emotional space between the participants. They are butting their heads together!

By first diffusing the emotion, you create a sliver of room to manoeuvre. Next, you can begin to unpick the intellectual conflict.

Where are they differing in their thinking?

By doing this you will also notice areas of shared thought and tiny strands of possible collaboration that, later, can be woven together.

It also helps to hold any conversations about the conflict in a physically neutral space, so use an office that is free from either participant's baggage.

Create space to get the good feeling flowing again.

Mediate and collaborate

Having understood the conflict to the best of your ability, the next step is to bring the participants together and mediate between them.

By mediating you are making a deliberate intervention, with the purpose being to bring about reconciliation.

Here's how:

1. Describe the situation as objectively as possible, stating the positions of each participant as you perceive them. Make sure that everyone agrees with this description – you're already establishing common ground!

2. Then, clearly state that the aim is to achieve reconciliation and find a way forward together. Again, gain agreement with this objective.

3. Allow each participant to air their views using non-accusatory language. The best way to do this is to ask them to use 'I' statements, for example: 'I feel that I can't approach you to discuss my workload.' As opposed to 'you' statements, for example: 'You are unapproachable and you never have any time to listen to my difficulty with the workload.' You can see how 'you' statements are provocative!

4. Look to build collaboration by generating ideas chains. In improvisation, the cardinal sin is to block your fellow improviser. Blocking occurs when you continually say no to your partner's ideas. Eventually, your partner becomes angry or gives up. Once the initial emotion has been diffused in a conflict, begin to unblock the communication by encouraging participants to build on each other's ideas. 'Yes, and. . . ' is a simple but powerful phrase. Ask the participants to listen to each other and respond by building on each other's ideas using 'yes. . . and'. For example: 'Perhaps we could schedule a biweekly meeting to talk about the work flow?' 'Yes and we could hold it in this neutral office.' Subtle changes in conversational habits, such as this, can have a long-lasting, transformative impact.

Refocus on the task at hand

The fact is, at work there is a job to be done. The demands of the project are paramount.

If all else fails, remind the participants in the conflict that there is a shared responsibility to get the job done.

Assert the needs of the project.

Focus on the facts.

Focus on the task.

Remind them of this shared challenge, and unite them in striving to achieve it.

How do I influence someone who's senior to me whom I never meet?

Tricky, but not impossible. Perhaps because you never actually meet you'll never have a direct influence on them, but you can try!

Find out everything you can about them. Take opportunities to join working groups, attend seminars and networking meetings where you'll be mixing with the person's colleagues. Hopefully in this way you'll at least have the opportunity to meet these colleagues, and, with the right preparation, impress with your vibrant working personality, attitude and ideas. Fellow workers should always be able to put a name to a face that you can approach.

Remember to play the long game and build alliances; identify those in your spheres who can help you with your influencing need and gain strength from this.

Tips to influencing 'big'

Read up

Knowledge is key here. Know all you can about the person you want to influence and their journey through the organisation. Consider where your need to influence fits into the bigger picture of the organisation.

Work 360°

Plan and continually refine your strategy to have an influence up, down and across the organisation. Strength comes in numbers. Select those who get the job done – if you can get them on board and being vocal it can do wonders. Once they are on board, work with them and meet regularly to check your strategy is paying off!

Connect

Consider how you can use LinkedIn/Twitter (or internal systems) – if you can connect on these platforms and others you can plan a strategy of awareness. You can use focused social networking to select interesting and useful articles and posts, thereby reinforcing your connection and increasing the chance of coming under their radar. Learn all you can about digital networking. Read Adam Gray's *Brilliant Social Media* to improve your skills in this area.

How do I influence someone reluctant to shift?

Most people don't enjoy change. Change can be perceived as a threat as it generates uncertainty about the future.

Humans are creatures of habit, and habits provide a sense of safety. How many times have you heard the phrase 'But we've always done it this way'? It's the cry of someone desperately clinging to the status quo, sometimes with good reason but at other times simply because they're not feeling good about change.

Tips to encourage someone to shift

Understand their reluctance

As with all influencing situations, understanding is essential. Their reluctance to move could manifest in a variety of behaviours: silence, anger, confrontation, vocal disagreement, rebellion.

You must look beyond the behaviour to the underlying emotion and empathise. Empathy with feelings of anxiety and fear about change is the only way to get things moving.

Having understood the deep-seated emotional response, you can then move on to understanding the finer detail of their reluctance.

What specifically do they dislike about the proposed changes? Once you get them communicating, you're on your way.

Ask open questions

If you go in too hard when someone is digging in their heels, you risk forcing them even further into their rut.

Direct challenges put people on the defensive, so try to avoid asking 'why' questions to begin with; for example:

- 'Why should we keep the existing system?' could be perceived as a demand for them to justify their ideas.

Instead, probe with open questions to gently encourage their position to soften; for example:

- 'What do you like about the current system?'
- 'What improvements would you suggest?'

Paint possible futures

When you're asking someone to change a particular behaviour, or change a working practice, it's essential to provide a new future for them to move in to.

More than likely, if they are very unconvinced about a particular change, they will, in their imagination, have created a negative future. In this future, all the good things about the old system will have been lost, they will feel powerless and nothing will work as well as it once did.

You need to counteract this negative vision by providing a convincing positive potential future.

Place your reluctant colleague at the heart of this future by using 'we' and 'you'.

For example:

> 'We will be able to produce the same results much more quickly and you will find your personal day-to-day workload reduced by about 25 per cent. This means you will have more time to spend on developing the business.'

149

Persuading someone to change first their feelings, then their opinion and finally their behaviour can be a slow process. But never forget, everyone is malleable and able to change in the end, no matter how much they say they don't want to.

You have to play the long game!

How do I remain credible at all times?

Do you believe yourself? Are you invested in your influencing need? Have you lost your way a little and become uncertain of your 'cred' (*slang)?*

Stop and return to the need. Decide in no uncertain terms why there is this need to influence and why you are the one to push it forward.

If you've carried out the exercises in Step 5, then you know that:

Credibility = Positive purpose + Skills + Qualities

and you are well on your way to moving from shaky to solid ground. From this ground, consider that when you communicate, any subconscious wavering of beliefs will show in the non-verbal cues you display. Much stress will manifest from feeling that you are not being entirely truthful in terms of either knowledge or belief. Therefore, having clarified your positive purpose, you must understand:

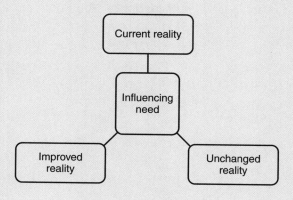

To get a grip on this, try not to ask yourself too many questions but perhaps start with:

What is driving the need?

Tips to remaining credible

Pay attention to yourself

Notice when you are feeling on shaky ground in terms of belief or knowledge. Do your homework and truly know your stuff.

Be congruent

Aim to communicate in a state of 'relaxed aliveness'. You are calm, you are grounded, your breath is centred and you are believable. Tension in the voice or body does not get in the way of your message. Your voice and body (all the non-verbal aspects of communication) work together – congruently. Body language works in clusters, so your tone of voice must not contradict your stance or your facial expression. If you are purposefully connected to 'the need' and in the relaxed state then all of this will tend to happen naturally.

It's your story

Trust yourself. Remember your personal experience is valid.

Tell *your* story. Follow your instincts. You know more than you imagine.

How do I ensure my influence has the required impact?

Throughout this book we have talked constantly about making the most of your personal impact, but it's worth repeating a few key ideas. If you take nothing more from this book, these ideas will ensure you make a good impression.

Tips to ensure your influence has impact

Everyone always has an impact

There is no avoiding making an impact. Even if you make no choices and take no control of your personal impact, you will still have one.

Even if you opt to lock yourself in your office and avoid all direct communication with other people, you will still have an impact.

Work always requires interaction with others, even if you're just sending an email, therefore there is simply no way of avoiding making some kind of impact on someone.

Given this, you may as well *make a choice*. Decide what you would like your impact on others to be.

For example, if you're feeling a bit irritable, and you have only one moment of communication with a colleague during that day, unless you have consciously decided to have a different impact you are likely to pass on your irritability, or even worse lead them to believe you are irritated with them!

For professional interactions, always consciously consider your impact.

Be specific

In Step 6 we suggested using active verbs to clarify your intention and impact. *Use them!* They focus your mind and body on a single, specific impact. Before a meeting, a pitch, a presentation, an interview or even just a conversation, choose a verb.

For example, do you want to make your colleague feel. . .

informed, excited, challenged, calmed, relieved, inspired, motivated, reassured or tickled?

Get a dictionary and expand your verb vocabulary; the more you have at your fingertips the finer your influencing skills will become.

Listen

Listening is probably the primary influencing skill. By remembering to listen to others you don't become domineering and accidentally negate the chance of making the positive impact you desire.

If people don't listen, it's all that is remembered about them. It puts people's noses out of joint, it rubs people up the wrong way, it closes people down. Not listening is not good enough.

Listening ensures you retain the right to make your impact.

Let it go

Finally, let it go. There's only so much you can do. You can't control what other people think or feel about you. You can only influence it, so once you have prepared properly and practised your communication you then need to relax a little.

You need drive, purpose and impact, but you also need ease, balance and flexibility.

It's yin and yang. One supports, and regulates, the other.

How do I influence when I'm under pressure?

What is the source of the pressure? Is it time? Do you need sign-off from a client on a project? Do you have your boss breathing down your neck? Do you need to get buy-in from team members to meet a deadline?

How is this pressure affecting you? If it is really starting to stress you out and have a physical/emotional effect on you, *stop*. More haste, less speed.

Take a moment to work out just how you will either deal with the pressure and soldier on, or how you can delegate or use your relationships to help you out. You should at this point be aware of Robert Cialdini's law of reciprocity – look him up, he's everywhere!

The simple question to ask yourself is 'Do you have any favours owed?'. Have you helped someone out in the past (have you allowed another to influence you) and now they feel obliged to help you? With influencing you must always think to the future and work to cultivate relationships where reciprocity is the norm. Then the next time you are under pressure there will be a valve to let some of that pressure off.

Tips for influencing under pressure

Give in

When you can, allow yourself to be influenced. Be seen and known to be flexible and agreeable. This can help build alliances and relationships that you can call upon should the need arise.

Go large

Otherwise known as 'door in the face', this can be particularly useful when under pressure. Increase the desired outcome from your influencing need. This way, when you scale down the outcome and the demands on those involved they'll be more open and willing to accommodate. For example:

You say you need the reports in by the end of the week but actually the end of the month will do; you need 15 images Photoshopped for your presentation tomorrow but actually five will do; you want to take the whole of June off but actually two weeks will be fine!

Stay centred

Return to your centred breath. It will stabilise you and ease away the panic.

Make centred breathing a lifetime habit!

How do I ensure I influence positively?

This question, perhaps, encapsulates the entire purpose of this book.

We agree that we have an influence, for better or for worse, so here are the guiding principles to ensure that it is positive.

Tips for influencing positively

Right feeling

In any influencing situation, the person with the strongest emotional state defines the feeling of the communication. The way you feel has a more influential effect on others than what you say or do.

Work on your feelings. If you are aware that you have negative feelings towards a particular person or meeting, make sure that you have talked them through with somebody independent beforehand. You have to create a bit of space around them.

Self-reflection is vital. If you aren't feeling right about something, then you must get to the root of it.

Seek to begin any influencing communication in a positive emotional state.

Right intention

All behaviour begins with intention.

It is very hard to behave in one way while intending something else, and if you do try it you run the risk of alienating people as they will sense that you don't quite mean what you say.

People pick up on your intention, so clarify it before you attempt to influence and always be positive! Positive intention is vastly more powerful than negative when you want others to follow your lead.

By stating your intention positively you give people cues as to how you want them to behave, as opposed to criticising them for how they are behaving.

For example, consider the difference between:

To point out the mistakes in current sales practice.

And, more positively:

To inspire staff to use the new sales system.

By unifying your intention and your actions you harness your power to influence.

Right thought

Clarity and thoroughness of thought demonstrate depth of engagement and intelligence. The clearer and more developed your thinking on any issue, the greater your chances of influencing others.

Make sure you give time to thinking things through before you seek to influence!

Be purposeful

Have a positive purpose that informs your work. All the most influential people are purposeful. Without purpose you are adrift, constantly responding to the shifting currents.

Anchor yourself with an underlying purpose at all times.

Having a purpose gives you clarity and enables others to see you clearly.

Tune in

As always, listen, listen, listen.

Close down your broadcast speakers and switch on your receptive antennae.

The only way to influence is to understand, and the only way to understand is to tune in to the thoughts and feelings of others.

This is a habit that can be developed, so start now.

Right action

What you *do* comes as a result of what you think, feel and intend. Your actions are the external expression of your internal world. If you perfect these three elements, right action will follow.

By right action we mean action that is congruent with your purpose, and is based on a deep sensitivity to and understanding of others. It is the culmination of all the preceding points in this list.

Your actions always influence others; people observe you and read into your actions, they form as much of an impression of who you are by watching how you behave as they do through direct communication with you.

Prepare properly and allow that preparation to flow through your actions.

Right communication

Right communication is everything. To communicate is to influence.

- Be yourself: be authentic, speak from your heart.
- Stay centred: be calm, balanced, embody ease.
- Listen: listen with a deep desire to understand.
- Empathise: show you understand both thoughts and feelings.
- Be flexible: adapt your communication style to meet the needs of each individual.

The skills and ideas in this book take time to develop. While some of the tips may act as quick fixes, to truly assimilate the techniques, and make them an automatic feature of your work practice, you will need to revisit the exercises at regular intervals over a three–six month period.

To achieve lasting change takes a little bit of work and dedication, which can, when the workload is stacking up, be difficult to maintain.

One of the best ways of ensuring that you stick to your development plan, guaranteeing that this book has a lasting positive impact, is to work with a buddy: a training partner.

Your training partner can be anyone who knows you well at work, or someone with an interest in helping you to develop. You could work with a colleague who is also keen to build their influencing skills; or, and perhaps ideally, you could work with your line manager or someone who is senior to you – a mentor.

While working with a colleague provides the perfect opportunity to both learn and develop your coaching skills in partnership, working with a manager means that the full focus of the sessions is on you and your influencing abilities. It also gives you the chance to build a relationship with someone senior to you, thereby increasing your ability to influence up the hierarchy, which isn't always easy.

With everyone's schedules full to the brim, it can be tricky to find a buddy willing to set aside the half an hour a week to work with you, so think strategically about who you ask, and what's in it for them. Influence them!

For example, many managers need to demonstrate their ability to nurture staff and bring their skills on, so working as your buddy would be a great opportunity for them to add some coaching experience to their CV.

This is how to do it

Working with your training partner will provide you with opportunity for:

- personal reflection;
- skill development;
- strategy.

Personal reflection

Never underestimate the value of personal reflection. Time spent discussing your experiences and workplace relationships is always useful, and sharpens your sense of identity and understanding. Through targeted conversation you drill down into your own experiences and begin to tap into the conditions that lie at the heart of everything you do. You bring more of yourself into your own awareness. You reduce your blind spots.

You may discover:

- helpful/unhelpful patterns of behaviour;
- hidden motivators;
- strengths/areas for development;
- interesting relationships;
- causes of anxiety;
- springs of inspiration;
- sources of energy/enthusiasm/interest;
- roots of fears/concerns.

A very simple way to enter personal reflection is to begin with a question. Your training partner could ask:

'What has gone well for you recently?'

'What have you found difficult recently?'

'Who are you working with at the moment? How's it going?'

'Has anything interesting struck you since we last met?'

And then, simply, follow your nose. Don't try to find a solution, just explore the response that arises.

A good way to avoid 'solving' a situation is for your training partner to refrain from asking 'why?'

Instead, use less-leading questions such as: 'Can you tell me more about that?' or 'What was that like for you?'.

Here we are not focusing on direct analysis, which tends to lead to over intellectualising, but on reflecting on personal experience, which can lead to insight.

Skill development

Skills are discrete, performable techniques. Often, a skill is the observable outcome of years of development, refinement and groundwork. For example, playing a perfect forehand in a game of tennis is a discrete skill borne out of hours of fitness work and racket control, analysis of the structure and shape of the game, development of a competitive personality and a meaningful relationship with the pleasure attributed to striking the ball cleanly. The skill is the tip of the iceberg.

Use this time with your training partner to develop specific skills, but remember that your ability to influence relies heavily on the depth and sincerity of your personality. The groundwork is essential.

Strategy

Working with a partner is the perfect opportunity to discuss your long-term goals and ambitions, and to plot the best possible route to achieve them.

Strategy is about turning your ideas into reality, into action, into things you can actually do.

Begin by defining your goals, for example: 'To be CEO by the time I'm 30!'. (There's nothing like aiming high.)

Then use a timeline, beginning at the present day and ending with your stated goal.

First, plot the **main events** that must occur on your way to your goal, for example 'Get promoted after one year at my current level'.

There should be three or four main events spread evenly over the timeline.

Next, look at the main event that is closest to the present day and plot the actions you need to take now, over the next week, over the next month and over the next three months.

The key is to plan and take short-term steps within a long-term framework.

You'll need to revisit your strategy every time you meet your training partner, both to check that the actions are being taken and to tweak your approach. Never be afraid to change your strategy!

Getting started

We would, of course, suggest that both you and your training partner have read the book before you begin working together. However, if that isn't possible the key is to have read one step per session, and work through the main steps in 10 sessions.

We always avoid being too prescriptive as to how people should use the book or any of the learning from our training courses, as there is no set formula, but it is essential that both you and your training partner have a shared language and grasp of the concepts. Otherwise, you'll spend the whole session reading the step!

Sometimes, when running coaching, a good starting point is to look over the table of contents and score each step in terms of priority: 10 being top, 1 being bottom.

If both you and your training partner do this independently, you will immediately have an interesting starting point. You may find that your training partner has a very different view of where your strengths lie, or you may find that the same clear areas for development are identified by both of you. Whatever the outcome, you will have a two-sided (your side and their side) snapshot of your current position, which is essential for setting you off in the right direction.

You can then work through the steps and the exercises within them in the order that best matches your developmental needs.

Of course, you can simply work through the steps in the order they are written, and all will make sense!

A suggested beginning: sessions 1-3

Your ability to influence rests on a combination of your skills and personality working within a defined context. The context is defined both by external factors – your place of work, the people around you and your role, and internal factors – your goals, your self-belief, your motivation and your values.

We would suggest that this context, these external and internal factors, are a good place to begin your sessions with your training partner.

1.   Complete your personal goals timeline as mentioned above.
2.   Use Step 5 to identify your positive purpose and firmly establish your own sense of credibility.
3.   Use Step 1 to map out your current workplace universe and audit all the central relationships within it.

In doing this you orientate both your internal compass and the external map over which you are moving.

Working with a more senior manager as your training partner is an excellent opportunity for deepening your understanding of your universe of influence. Your manager will be able to make suggestions as to how you can nurture the relationships and help you identify the key people to draw further into your orbit. The old adage 'It's who you know, not what you know' has more than a ring of truth to it.

Don't rush this work. These first steps are likely to take at least 2–3 sessions to complete.

Next: sessions 4-6

Target the skills that you and your training partner feel are most pertinent to your needs and focus on one skill per session.

It is important that you and your partner are willing to try the exercises out. Don't just sit there and read about them! It is all too easy to read the instructions and think to yourself, 'That seems easy'.

Just because it looks as if the exercises are easy, don't be fooled. You have to have a go at them and see what arises as a result. You will only deepen your self-knowledge and build new skills by stretching yourself and by opening up to discovery.

Try each exercise a few times. Make sure your partner gives you feedback in between each attempt. You will learn these skills incrementally. The big mistake is to opt out and assume that simply by reading about them, you have learnt them.

It is advisable to repeat these skills sessions cyclically. You may, for example, have identified communication skills as a key area of development. In which case, your programme could look like this:

Session 4: use Step 2 to work through the breath, eye contact and physical alignment exercises, while both standing and sitting.

These exercises may result in a feeling of falling apart! You are, after all, breaking your communication skills into distinct components that you are used to using without too much thought.

Session 5: use Step 3 to work through the breathing, tone and articulation exercises. Make sure you do the self-recording too, as this will help you understand the quality of your voice better. Save the recording for later reference!

Again, you are breaking your voice down into its constituent parts here, so you may suddenly find the sound of your own voice a little alien. It's all part of the process.

Session 6: use Step 8 and try the listening, empathy and presence exercises. You will find that the non-verbal and vocal skills worked on in the previous sessions feed directly into this session. This session provides the perfect chance to try to put all of your communication skills into action together.

In between all of these sessions make sure you are subtly applying the skills to your daily life. Don't just forget about them!

Eventually, they will settle into subconscious use, but at this early stage you need to keep them firmly in the foreground.

Lastly: sessions 7-9

Repeat the cycle. Rerun sessions 4–6. You'll find that the skills have settled a little, and that you are slowly beginning to put them together to form a coherent whole.

Don't be tempted to skip these revisiting sessions. You are not 'going over old ground', you are returning to make sure all the seeds you planted in earlier sessions are taking root.

You will also find that the exercises are worth returning to. Each run of them is different, fresh and alive, as all communication should be.

Repetition is an important part of the learning process. This is not a tick-box training programme, you are never 'qualified' or 'certified'. This training is more like yoga, a sport or an art where you return to the same postures and exercises week after week and deepen your understanding of them.

Parallel case studies

Finally, we often find that the case studies in Part 1, and the real-life contexts described in Parts 2 and 3, highlight useful parallels from a trainee's life.

We'd like you and your training partner to regard this book as unfinished. After all, influencing is an open-ended skill set, there's nothing you can't add to your tool box.

As part of your training, imagine you are providing the case study for each step, drawing it from your own experience. Your training partner can also offer case studies from their experience, sharing the benefit of their career with you.

This may sound like a laborious task, but it needn't be. You can discuss these case studies with your training mentor for as long or short a time as you wish.

The key is to apply the concepts in the book to your own experience, to see them in action in your life. By re-imagining each step's case study, you will be required to review your own experience with a specific influencing skill focus in each case.

Through doing this you will not only see how the skills are seamlessly woven into your everyday life, but also how to start to use them for greater effect.

Finally, enjoy!

Communication should always be enjoyable . . . even when it is difficult. All communication is an attempt to both understand and be understood, and, following that, to have a positive effect on those around you – to influence them for the better.

Use your sessions with your training partner to find the fun in communication. A smile, even laughter, should never be too far from your lips in these sessions . . . and if it is, find a new training partner as quickly as you can.

As we suggested at the start of this book, it is a good idea to reassess your skills and, crucially, your confidence in using those skills now that you have completed the influence workout.

Remember: this workout is not necessarily a quick fix. You may need to revisit certain steps time and again until they feel like a habit to you. Learning new skills can happen quickly, but deep personal change takes a lot longer to settle in.

Use this questionnaire as the starting point for your continued personal and professional development.

Re-score yourself 1–10 for each of these questions, with 10 indicating a high level of confidence and skill and 1 a low level:

1. **How influential do you feel at work?**

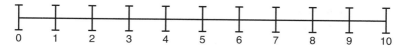

2. **How influential do you feel at home?**

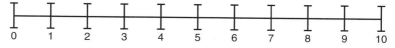

3. **How well do you understand your universe of influence/ network of relationships?**

4. **How comfortable are you using non-verbal communication?**

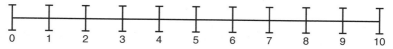

5. How confident are you in the sound of your voice?

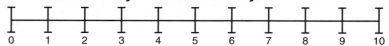

6. How comfortable are you when presenting to an audience?

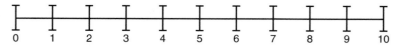

7. How confident are you at reading the signals others give?

8. How assertive are you?

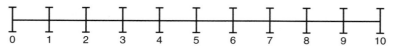

9. How readily do you speak your mind at work?

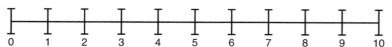

10. How purposeful do you feel at work?

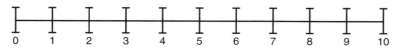

11. How easily could you state your core values?

12. How comfortable are you when talking to senior colleagues?

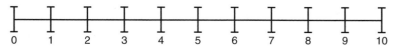

13. How would you rate your listening skills?

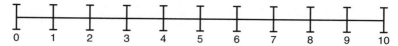

14. How effectively do you put your thoughts into words?

15. How confident are you in your goals and the actions you need to take to achieve them?

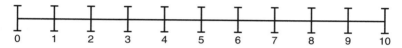

Once you have read the book, completed all the exercises more than once and spent some time working on the techniques with a training partner mentor, take the questionnaire again and notice in which areas you have developed significantly and which still require attention.

Ideally, you should set yourself five clear, achievable influencing goals and work towards them over the next six months or so. Make sure you check in regularly with this questionnaire to monitor your progress.

Remember: becoming influential doesn't happen overnight, it's a lifelong project!

Set your next five influencing goals now

1.

2.

3.

4.

5.

Do you want your people to be the very best at what they do?

Talk to us about how we can help.

As the world's leading learning company, we know a lot about what your people need in order to be better at what they do.

Whatever subject or skills you've got in mind (from presenting or persuasion to coaching or communication skills), and at whatever level (from new-starters through to top executives) we can help you deliver tried-and-tested, essential learning straight to your workforce – whatever they need, whenever they need it and wherever they are.

Talk to us today about how we can:

- Complement and support your existing learning and development programmes
- Enhance and augment your people's learning experience
- Match your needs to the best of our content
- Customise, brand and change it to make a better fit
- Deliver cost-effective, great value learning content that's proven to work.

Contact us today:
corporate.enquiries@pearson.com